W9-CLB-149

From Flower to Fruit

Anne Ophelia Dowden

FROM FLOWER TO FRUIT

Illustrated by the Author

THOMAS Y. CROWELL NEW YORK

ACKNOWLEDGMENTS

In collecting the hundreds of specimens on which these drawings are based, I have had the help of friends and acquaintances throughout the country—so many that I can thank most of them only collectively. I am, however, particularly indebted to the following: Mr. and Mrs. Albert Van Vlack, Canaan, Conn.; Mr. and Mrs. Frederick McGourty, Norfolk, Conn.; Mrs. Gertrude Foster, Falls Village, Conn.; Miss Constance Campbell, Lime Rock, Conn.; Dr. Peter Dykeman, Cary Arboretum, Millbrook, N.Y.; Mrs. Lorraine Barstow, Norfolk, Conn.; Mr. and Mrs. Henry Rockwell, Canaan, Conn.; Mrs. Phyllis Busch, Lakeville, Conn.; Mr. and Mrs. Stuart Eldredge, Springfield, Vt; Dr. Eville Gorham, Minneapolis, Minn.; Dr. James Zimmerman, Madison, Wisc.; Mrs. Kathryn Nalody, Minneapolis, Minn.; and Mr. John Moore, Denver, Colo.

The Brooklyn Botanic Garden provided me with both specimens and research information, and for these I want to thank Dr. Stephen K.-M. Tim, Mrs. Nancy Tim, Mr. Edmond Moulin, Mr. Thomas Dellendick, and Miss Marie Giasi. And above all, I am deeply indebtd to Dr. Peter K. Nelson, Professor of Botany, Brooklyn College, who read my manuscript, answered endless questions, and guided me patiently through many intricate botanical problems.

Designed by Harriett Barton
First Edition

Library of Congress Cataloging in Publication Data
Dowden, Anne Ophelia Todd, 1907–
From flower to fruit.

Includes index.
Summary: Text and botanical illustrations explain how flowers mature into seed-bearing fruits.
1. Plants—Reproduction—Juvenile literature. 2. Flowers—Juvenile literature. 3. Fruit—Juvenile literature. 4. Seeds—Juvenile literature. [1. Plants—Reproduction. 2. Flowers. 3. Fruit. 4. Seeds] I. Title.
QK827.D67 1984 582'.016'6 83-46163
ISBN 0-690-04402-X
ISBN 0-690-04403-8 (lib. bdg.)

ON A SEED

This was the goal of the leaf and the root.
For this did the blossom burn its hour.
This little grain is the ultimate fruit.
This is the awesome vessel of power.

For this is the source of the root and the bud—
World unto world unto world remolded.
This is the seed, compact of God,
Wherein all mystery is enfolded.

Georgie Starbuck Galbraith
The New York Times, May 6, 1960

To the memory of my husband, Raymond Dowden, who for so many years tramped the fields and woodlands with me, helped to solve the practical problems of plant collecting, and shared the delights and surprises that reward all those who probe the marvelous perspectives of the green world.

Contents

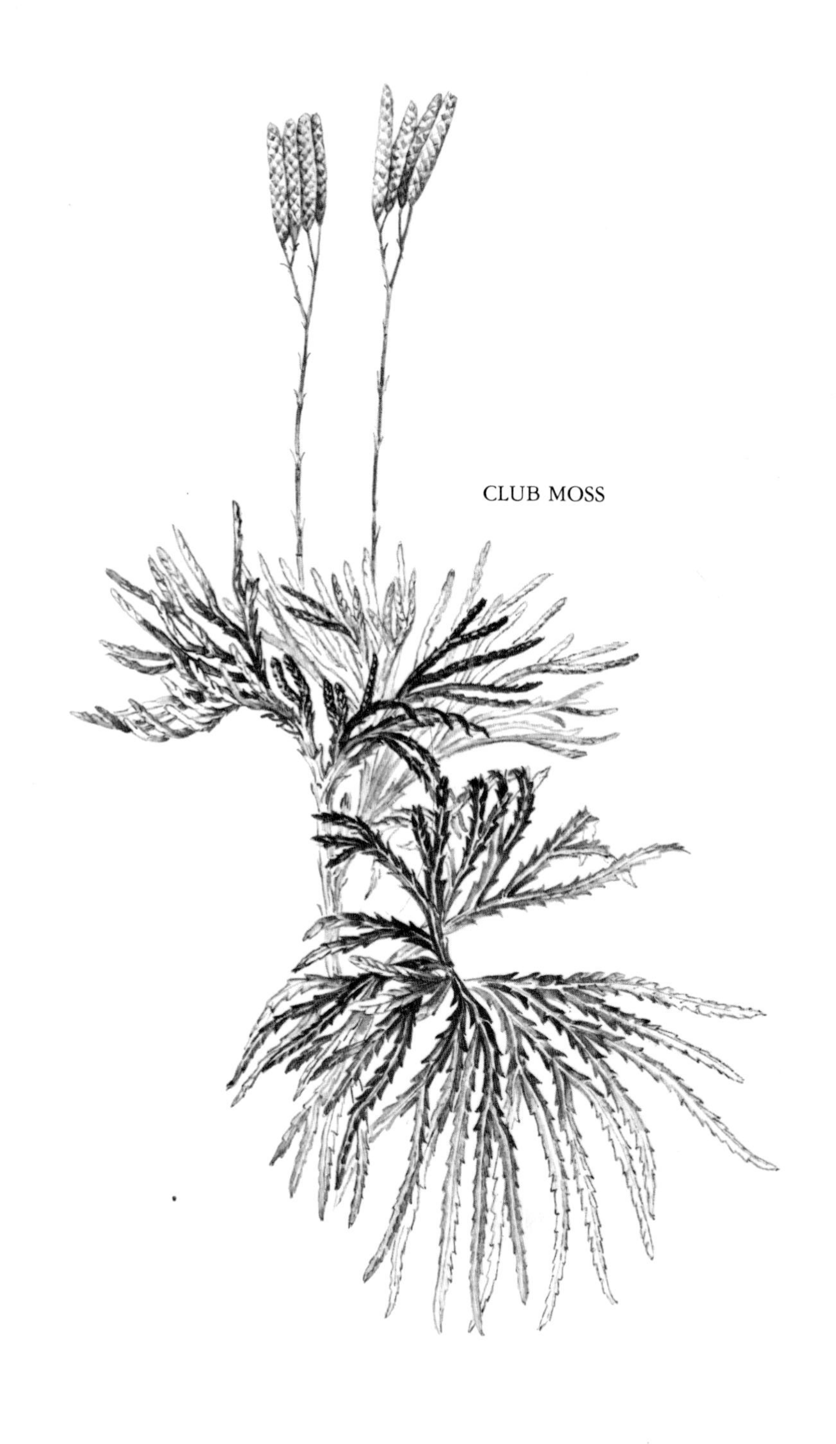

CLUB MOSS

HOW SEEDS CHANGED THE WORLD

Through most of its four and a half billion years, our planet has been a desolate place. Volcano-torn and bleak, its rocky surface bore no green at all for countless ages, and only during the last 100 million years or so has the land been covered with a rich and varied mantle of plants. About 3 billion years ago, life began to develop in the oceans, and from minute one-celled organisms that could scarcely be called either plant or animal came a wealth of forms that gradually filled the seas. But the land remained barren.

As eon followed eon, small marine algae began to live on the edges of seas and inlets; and when they had evolved coverings that could keep them from drying out, they were able to spread, like strips of green carpet, into the landscape of bare rock. But they were all tied inevitably to rivers and swamps, because their means of reproducing themselves depended on water. These ancient plants were very similar to the algae and mosses of today. Their reproductive process involved microscopic swimming male sperms that had to wriggle their way through water to reach and fertilize the female eggs. Also, since they had neither roots nor stiff stems, these plants lay on the ground or just below it and could exist only in a wet environment.

Gradually, other plants appeared, with roots that could reach down into the earth for water. These were the club mosses, horsetails, and ferns, not unlike the ones we have today except that they were able to grow to enormous size. During the age of the dinosaurs, these plants dominated the earth. Their strong woody stems enabled some of them to grow 90 feet tall, like the tree ferns of present-day tropics. Their dense groves were majestic, but they were surrounded by no grass, no daisies, no little forest plants. And in reproducing themselves, they still had to send their tiny sperms swimming to find female cells. This could be accomplished with rainwater or dew, but it was a serious disadvantage for plants with their heads so far above the ground.

Then, about 290 million years ago, the conifers appeared. The cells that produced their delicate sperms were enclosed in pollen grains that kept them from drying out. Borne in little cones, the pollen was released to the wind, which carried it till it reached eggs in other cones. This was a great innovation, freeing the plants from their bondage to water; but conifers made an even more important contribution to the evolution of the green world: An egg fertilized by pollen remained in the cone for a long time, while its cells accumulated a rich food supply and a waterproof coat grew around it—the seed had been born. When a cone finally dried and its segments opened, the seeds lying between them dropped to the ground. And there, if necessary, they could wait for years before they germinated and started to grow.

The very first seeds had evolved in the seed ferns, but these plants all vanished quickly—after only a few million years—whereas the conifers were a great success. They were able to march across the drier regions of the earth, and today, scarcely changed, they form about one third of all the forests of the world.

But reliance on wind for carrying pollen is always haphazard and wasteful. A pollen grain is effective only if it happens to fall on a female cone. So the plant must produce pollen in unbelievable quantities—often great clouds of it—much of which never reaches its goal. The world still needed a more efficient system for uniting male and female cells, and this system came with the flowering plants, so versatile and varied that they have all but taken over the vegetable kingdom. Now at last the green monotony of the conifer forests could be broken by a great diversity of herbs and vines and trees, and now a mantle of grass could spread over the bare plains.

Most flowering plants are pollinated by agents like insects, which carry small amounts of pollen and place it in exactly the spot where it will be effective. Originally, insects visited flowers for meals of pollen and incidentally carried some of it on their bodies as they flew to other flowers. Later, a new kind of food was added—nectar, which has no purpose except to attract pollinators. To advertise this bounty, flowers acquired large, bright-colored petals and a variety of scents.

And flowering plants are also fruiting plants. Though their new, efficient method of joining sperm and egg was very important, an equally profound innovation was the protection of the growing seed in the heart of the flower. The seeds of conifers are "naked"—unprotected and loosely held in the scales of the cones. The seeds of flowering plants are enclosed in ovaries that eventually become fruits, shielding the seeds during their development and often helping in their distribution when they are ripe.

Essentially seeds are baby plants packaged and protected and nourished until they can survive on their own, at first enclosed in fruits and eventually lying in the earth awaiting the signal to grow. They are really astonishing little things—flying and bouncing about the world, traveling in the fur of animals, spreading their species far and wide, and able to perpetuate their kind even years after their parents are dead and gone.

The appearance of flowering plants 120 million years ago paralleled dramatically the rise of birds and mammals, probably because these plants produced concentrated foods in a way that had never been known before. Active warm-blooded animals, with their agile brains, have a high oxygen consumption and need rich food, which the great lizards and other cold-blooded creatures could do without. Once the slow-motion world of reptiles and amphibians was left behind, the intensely active life of birds and mammals and man himself all depended, directly or indirectly, on the gift of seeds.

CHICKWEED

FLOWERS

In today's green world, there are about 200,000 species of flowering plants. They range from giant towering oak trees to tiny creeping chickweeds, but they all have the same basic parts. And however much these parts may vary in size and shape and position, each contributes to the growth and nourishment of the plant and to its final goal of reproducing itself with seeds.

The *roots* are anchors and, with their minute absorbent hairs, the means of gathering water and minerals from the earth. They also receive and store food manufactured by the leaves. *Stems* support the plant and contain tubes that carry food substances up and down. *Leaves* spread out to catch the sun, which acts on their green chlorophyll to turn carbon dioxide and water into the sugars, starches, and oils that nourish the plant. *Flowers* are the reproductive organs: they bear

A TYPICAL FLOWER

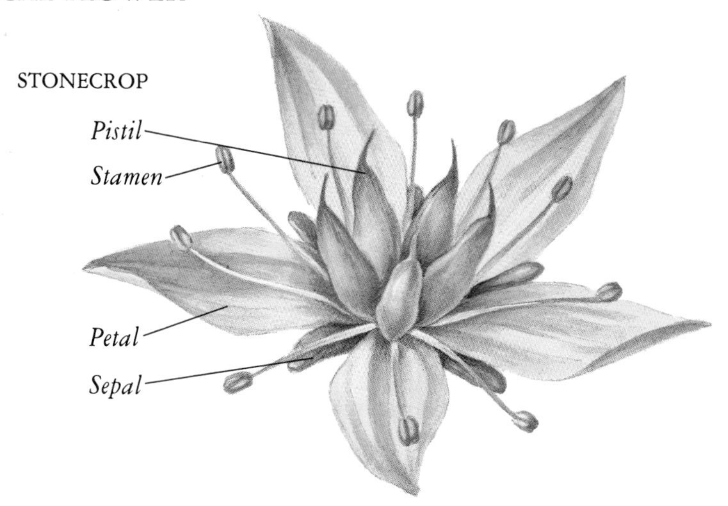

the male and female cells, shelter the growing seeds, and eventually produce fruits.

A typical flower has four sets of parts gathered together on a *receptacle*, which is merely the enlarged top of the stem. In the center of the flower are one or more *pistils* surrounded by a ring of *stamens*, then a ring of *petals*, and on the outside a ring of *sepals.* The petals as a group are called the *corolla*; the sepals form the *calyx.*

The calyx is commonly green, with leaflike sepals. Its primary purpose is to enclose and protect the unopened bud, but in some plants it has other functions as well, including protection and dispersal of seeds.

The corolla also shields the tender and vital inner flower parts, but its most important and dramatic duty is to attract various agents of pollination, provide them with landing plat-

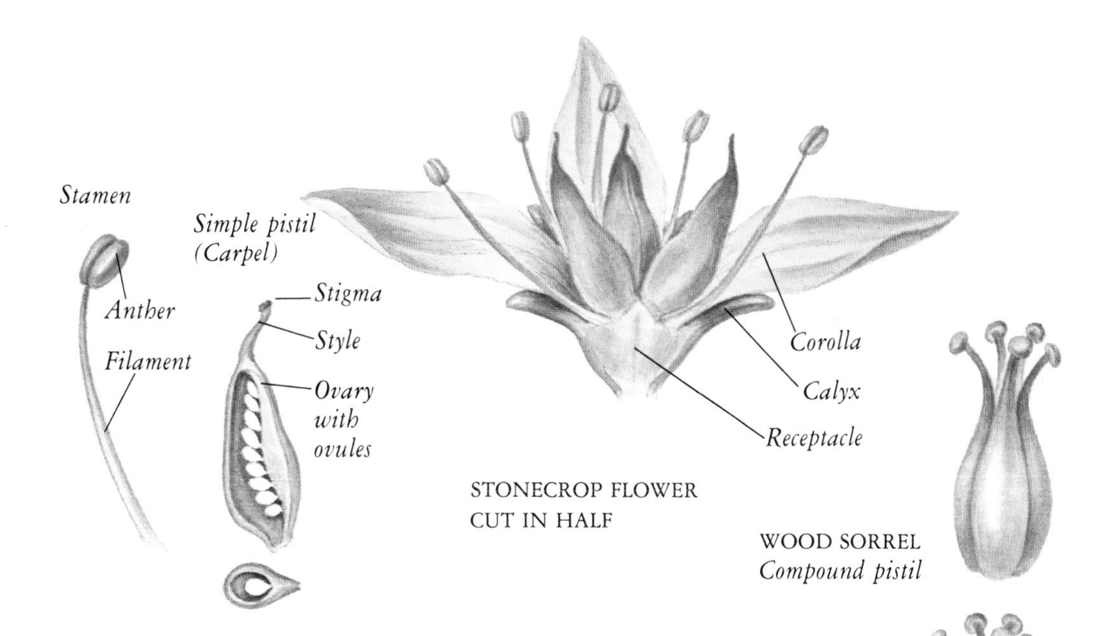

STONECROP FLOWER
CUT IN HALF

WOOD SORREL
Compound pistil

forms, and guide them to the pollen and nectar.

Stamens are the male parts of the flower. Their little sacs or *anthers* produce, store, and finally release the *pollen* grains that contain the male cells. These anthers are usually borne at the ends of thin stalks or *filaments.*

The pistils in the center are the female parts. Each pistil usually has three clearly visible sections: At its base is the *ovary*, a pouch containing *ovules* (the future seeds); above this rises a stalk or *style*, which carries at its top the *stigma*, a sticky or furry knob to catch and hold pollen. A basic *simple pistil* is called a *carpel.* In the stonecrop shown here, and in many other flowers, the carpels are all separate units, but very commonly carpels are joined together—several of them fused into a single body, a *compound pistil.*

Pistils and stamens do not always grow side by side in one

blossom, though that is by far the commonest arrangement. In some plants the pistils are in one flower, the stamens in another. Sometimes, as in the beech tree or castor bean plant, these *pistillate* and *staminate* flowers grow on the same branch; but sometimes, as in sassafras or meadow rue, they are on entirely separate plants.

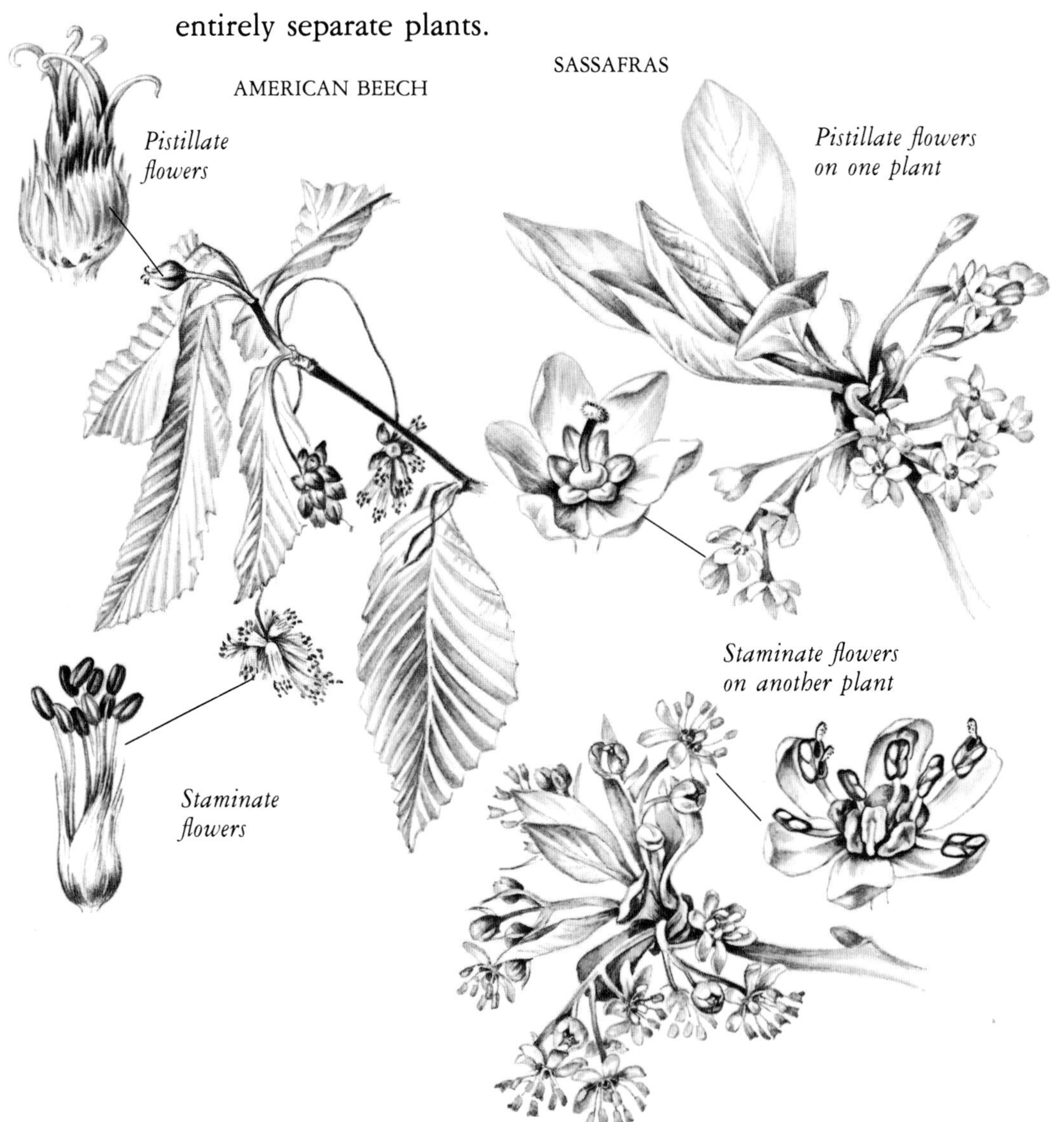

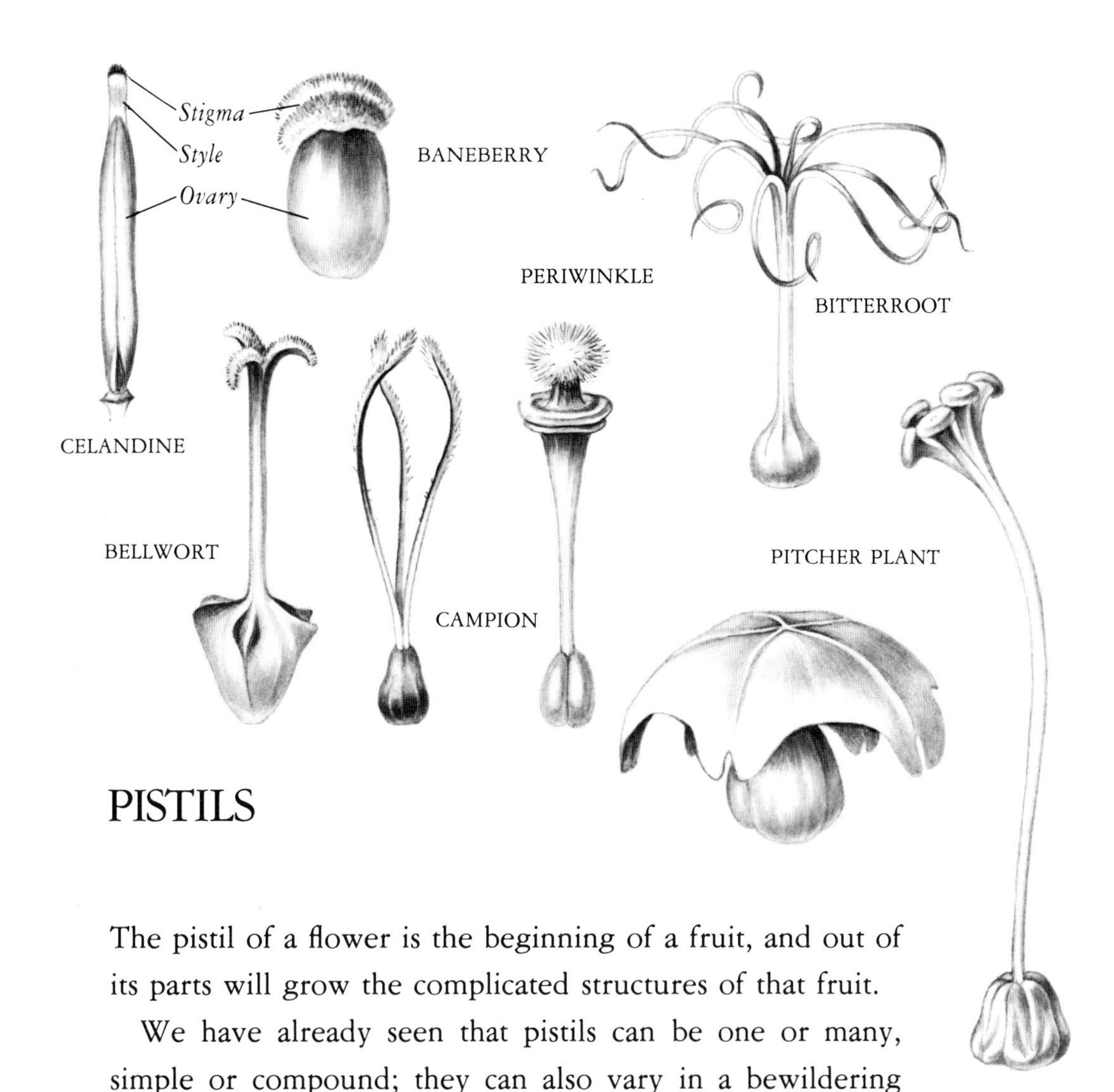

PISTILS

The pistil of a flower is the beginning of a fruit, and out of its parts will grow the complicated structures of that fruit.

We have already seen that pistils can be one or many, simple or compound; they can also vary in a bewildering number of other ways. Their ovaries may be balls or tubes or irregular pouches. Styles may be long or short, fat or thin, one or several—or even entirely missing. Stigmas can be tiny buttonlike knobs, flaring arms, or elaborate petallike forms; but they always have some kind of sticky or fuzzy surface to catch pollen.

MANY SIMPLE PISTILS

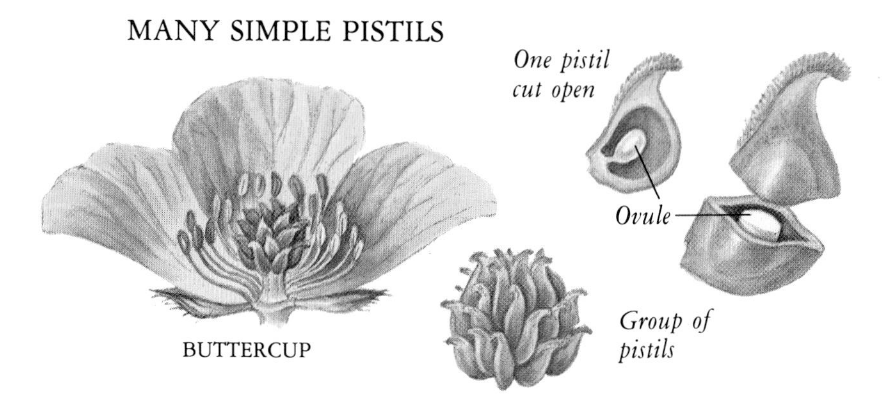

The earliest types of flowers were somewhat like the magnolia and the buttercup, with a very large number of one-carpel pistils. Many of these flowers still exist, but evolution has tended to reduce the number of pistils, and some flowers have ended up with only one. The cherry, for instance, has a single simple pistil—a single carpel containing two ovules. The garden pea also has one simple pistil, but it contains a whole row of ovules attached to its inner seam.

But in more than half of all flowering plants, the reduction

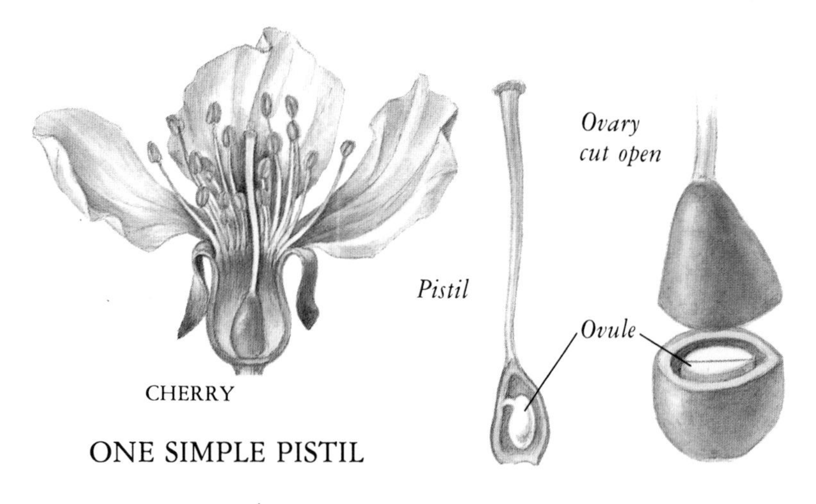

ONE SIMPLE PISTIL

ONE SIMPLE PISTIL

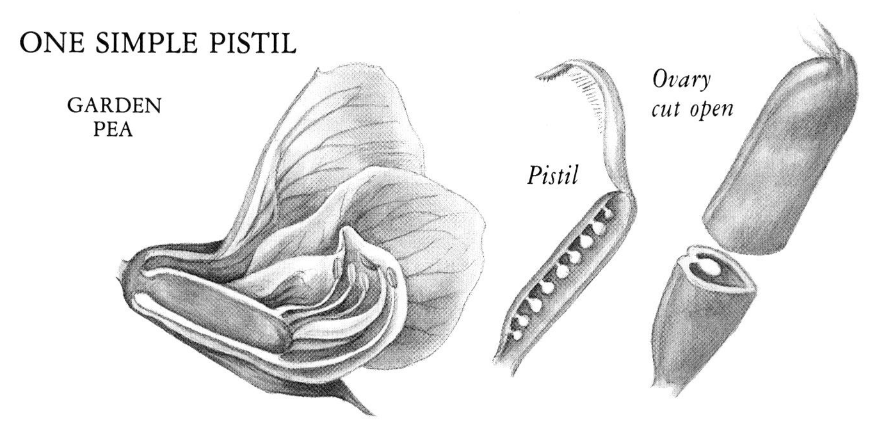

has been to a few carpels (two to five, or rarely more) joined into a single body, the compound pistil. They are so closely fused together that, at first glance, some compound pistils look exactly like the simple pistil of the cherry. But if we cut through the ovary of a compound pistil with a sharp knife, we can often quite distinctly see the carpels that formed the union. The compound pistil of a lily, for example, looks like three pea ovaries joined by their backbones. And sometimes the carpels are obvious without an incision, visible as bumps

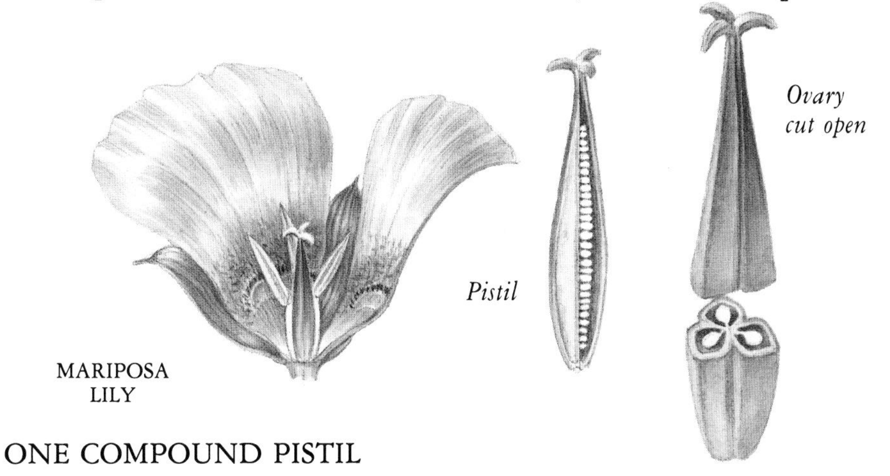

ONE COMPOUND PISTIL

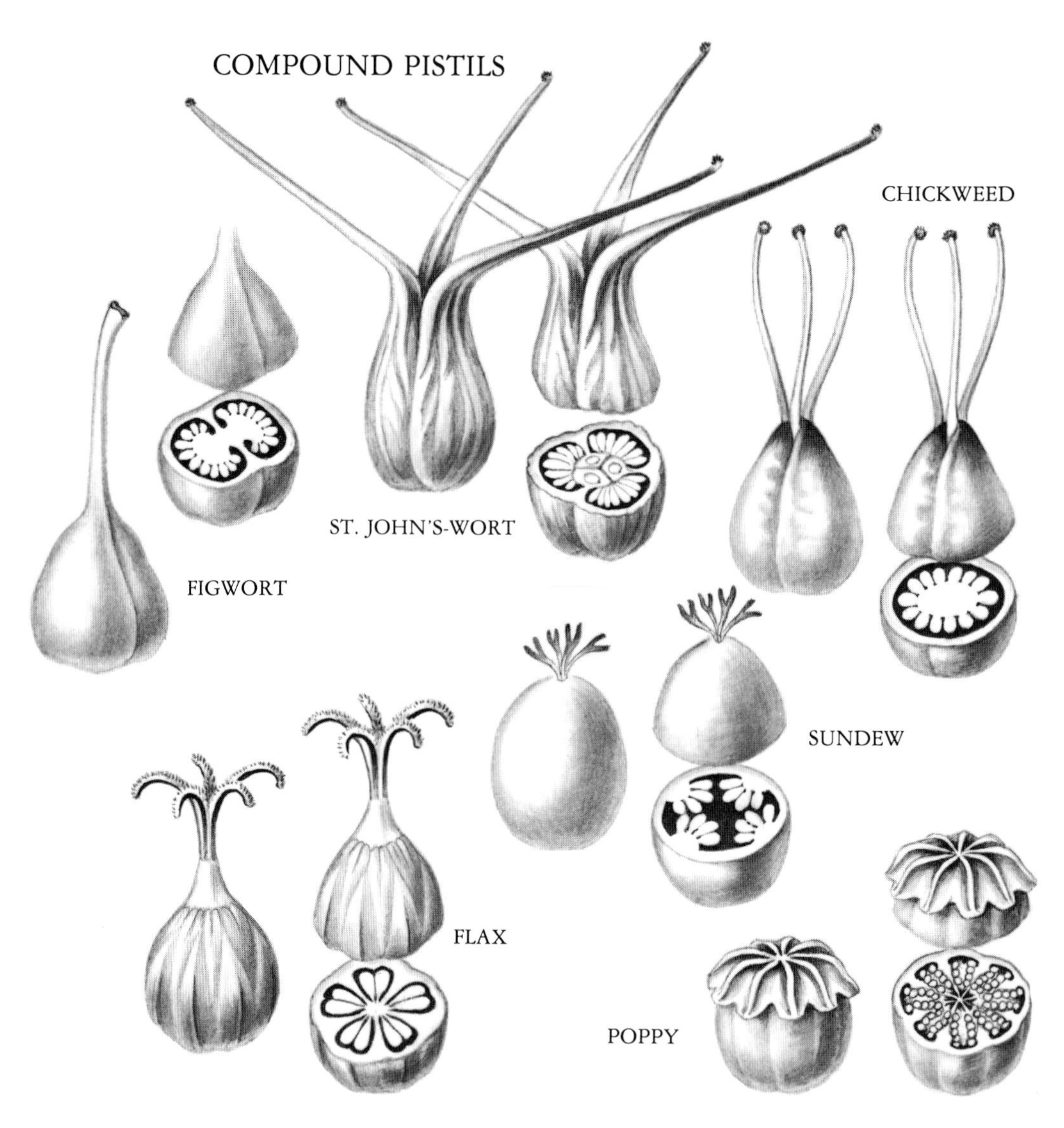

or grooves or stripes on the outside of the ovary.

Even inside the ovary, however, matters are not always clear. Though the basic carpel walls of many compound pistils are very distinct, like those of the lily, in some plants evolution has changed the shape of those walls or they have disappeared entirely or new partitions have appeared. The grouping of the ovules may give our only clue to the number of carpels that formed the compound ovary. But stigmas, and sometimes styles, can also be a guide, because the upper tips of carpels have generally remained separate even when the lower parts joined. Often they are spread out in a number of arms or lobes that matches the number of carpels in the compound ovary below them.

Ovaries are the fruits-to-be, and they may each contain one ovule or hundreds. The ovules may be arranged in many different ways: attached to the sides or bottom of the ovary wall, or to a center "pole," or to inner partitions. Each one grows on a little stalk, sometimes upright, sometimes bent so that the ovule hangs down. Each ovule usually has at least two layers of coating or *integument*, and at its center is the *embryo sac* containing the crucial cells that, after fertilization, will grow into a baby plant. This little package is the future seed.

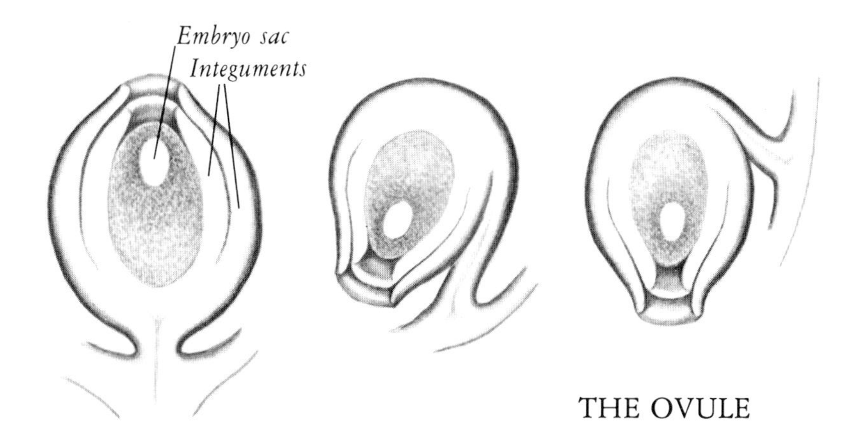

THE OVULE

INSECT POLLINATION
BUMBLEBEE ON
RED CLOVER
HONEYBEE ON
BORAGE
BUTTERFLY ON
MARJORAM

BURNET

A wind-pollinated flower, without petals

FERTILIZATION

All parts of a flower work together toward the final goal of seed production. All have important, well-defined roles, but in the last analysis only the stamens and pistils are absolutely essential. Male cells from stamens must reach and join, or *fertilize*, female cells in pistils to produce new individuals.

Since, in most flowers, anthers and stigmas grow side by side, a transfer of pollen from one to the other would seem very easy. This sometimes happens, but it has a serious drawback: the loss of a mixture of heredity. Only a union of cells from two separate individuals of the same species can bring together two different sets of genes. They can combine in many different ways and produce variations in offspring that may result in changes in the species. Much of the evolution of past ages has been the result of such change, and plant species still need it if they are to adapt to new environments. So flowers have a great many devices that hinder self-fertilization, or even prevent it completely.

If they are to receive pollen from other plants, flowers must rely on a great variety of couriers to transport it—bees, butterflies, beetles, and many other insects; birds, bats, and other animals; wind and water. These couriers do not do the job intentionally: Insects and animals visit flowers because they like to eat pollen or nectar or even petals; wind and water flow at random. But they all, unknowingly, pick up pollen in one flower and drop it off in another.

In insect-pollinated flowers we meet one of nature's most delicate and intricate relationships—advantageous to both flower and courier. To tempt these messengers, flowers display brilliant colors and alluring scents; sometimes petals with strange shapes or bright patterns guide the insect to its food by the pathway that will most surely leave it smeared with pollen. Thousands of insects and thousands of flowers have evolved together into this present-day fraternity, and some have become totally dependent on each other. Wind pollination, too, has affected the shapes of the flowers that rely on it—their petals and sepals are always small and inconspicuous or often missing altogether.

But here we are concerned only with what happens after pollination has occurred. We can forget about the glamorous petals—in fact, we can forget about every part of the flower except the pistil. When petals and stamens have served their purpose, they nearly always dry up and fall off. Often the sepals fall off too, though they do sometimes remain as part of the developing fruit.

The pistil, however, is just beginning its share of the drama. When pollen grains reach its stigma, they are caught and held in a sticky liquid. Stimulated by the sugary fluid, a tube breaks through the wall of each grain and pushes its way down through the style and into the ovary. Some of these tubes find ovules and enter them. Then the contents of the pollen grains flow down the tubes, leaving the empty shells on the stigma. Inside an ovule, the tip of a tube releases two sperms into the embryo sac, which contains several nuclei. One sperm fuses with an egg nucleus, fertilizing it and starting the growth of a new plant or *embryo.* The other sperm fuses with a pair of nuclei that develop into the *endosperm*—a food-storing tissue that surrounds and nourishes the embryo.

This completes fertilization: The ovule is now ready to grow into a seed and the ovary into a fruit. Usually, a fruit begins to grow as soon as even one ovule is fertilized, and if none are fertilized, there is no fruit at all. However, accidental plant mutations sometimes produce fruits without fertilization and therefore without seeds. Such plants can be propagated by cuttings, and in this way horticulturists have bred all the seedless varieties of oranges, bananas, and grapes we buy in our markets.

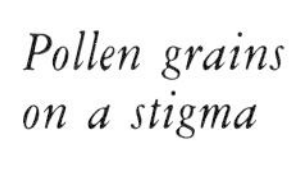

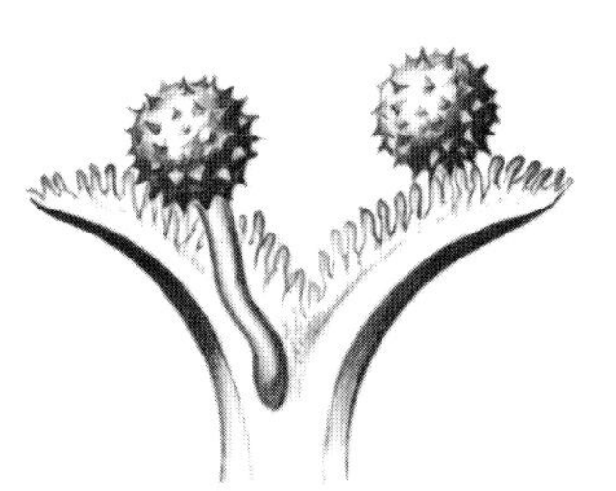

FERTILIZATION OF AN OVULE

FRUITS CALLED SEED PODS

Our fruit is now on its way. Its ovules are growing into seeds, and the ovary enclosing them is turning into the *pericarp* or seed vessel. All fruits are, basically, ripened ovaries. They may hold one seed or several or hundreds. They may open to release the ripe seeds, or remain closed so that the young plants have to penetrate the fruit walls when they start to grow. Fruits may be fleshy, like plums, or dry, like milkweeds, but most people recognize only the fleshy ones as "fruits" and are inclined to call the dry ones "seed pods."

Botanists call them all fruits, grouping them according to type and giving names to the groups—a system of classification that is rather complicated and not very interesting. What *is* interesting is the enormous number of ways in which the basic flower parts of various plants develop into a multitude of differing but efficient seed envelopes. These variations, with their endless surprises, are well worth investigating, and we may as well learn their scientific names as we go along.

As the ovary grows into a fruit, it sometimes changes very little in shape, but in most plants it does change—often dramatically. Parts of the pistil may disappear; other parts may expand disproportionately; the ovary wall may change from soft to leathery, as in the orange; to bony, as in the hazelnut;

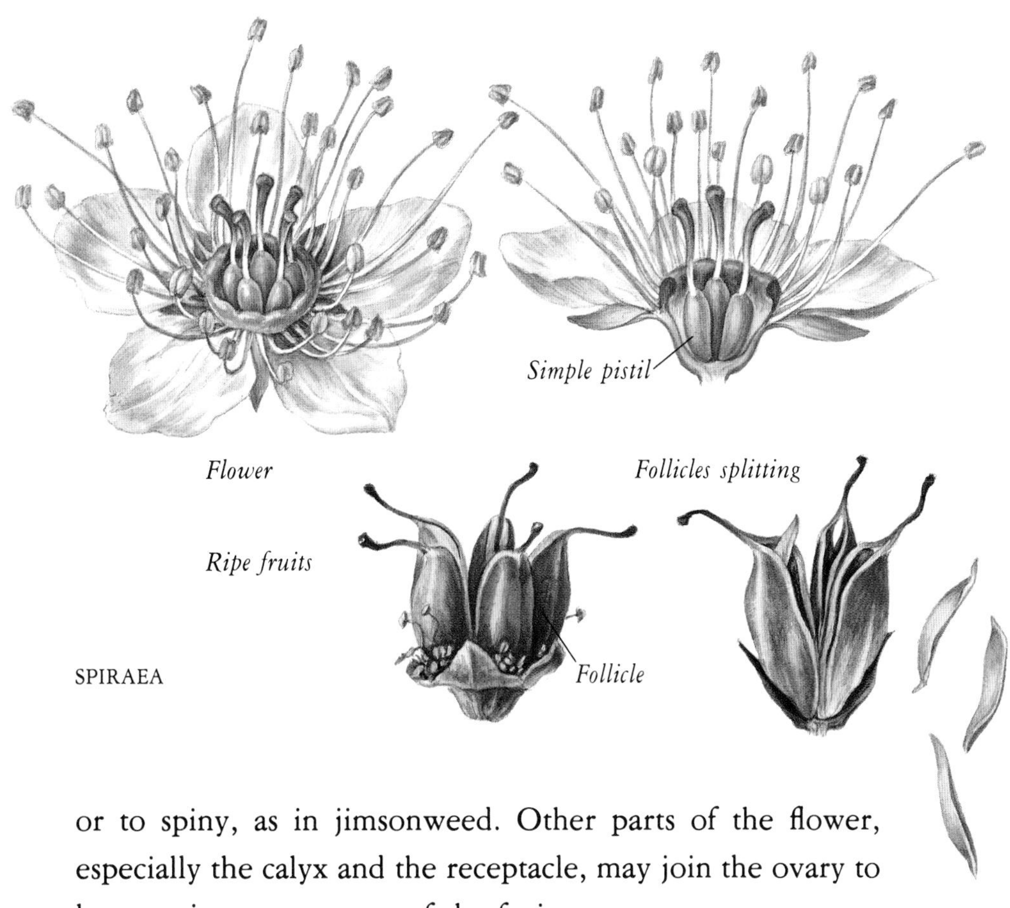

or to spiny, as in jimsonweed. Other parts of the flower, especially the calyx and the receptacle, may join the ovary to become important parts of the fruit.

The simplest fruits, of course, are those that develop from single carpels. But single-carpel fruits do not by any means all follow the same patterns as they grow. A spiraea flower has a cluster of five separate one-carpel pistils, and each pistil contains a number of seeds. When they are ripe, each dry pericarp splits from top to bottom down its inside seam, and the seeds are free to fall from the opening. This kind of fruit is called a *follicle.*

Follicles can be as tiny as those of spiraea or as large as

those of milkweed. They very often grow in clusters, matured from pistil clusters like the ones found in so many flowers of the buttercup and sedum families. But in the milkweed and dogbane families, they develop from a rather curious pair of simple pistils that are joined at the top by a single stigma. As the fruits grow, the stigma drops off and the two ovaries spread apart, to become two follicles that eventually split to release hundreds of tufted seeds.

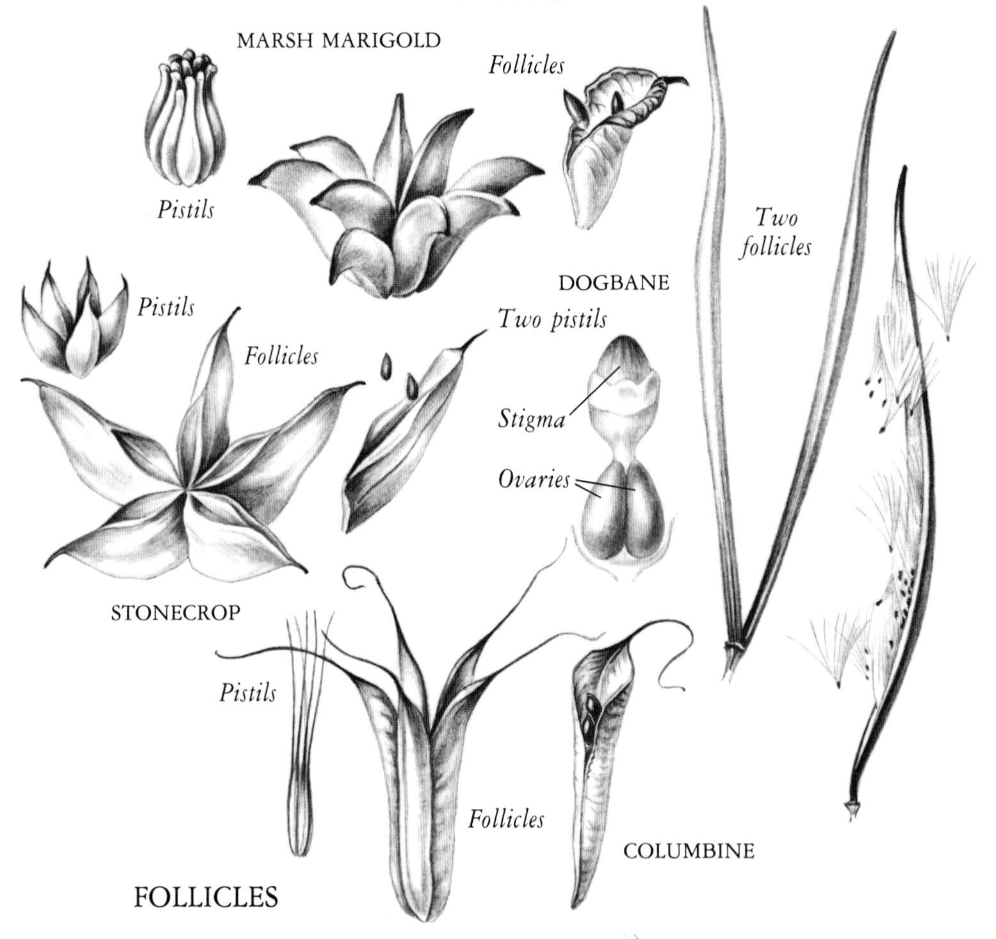

FOLLICLES

The rather similar one-carpel pod of the garden pea is called by a different name—*legume*—because it splits down both edges instead of along a single seam. Most members of the pea family bear legumes. They vary widely in size and shape, from the long flat pods of the honey locust to the tiny curled ones of alfalfa. And a few do not split in the normal way: Mimosa pods break crosswise into small sections, and peanuts do not open at all.

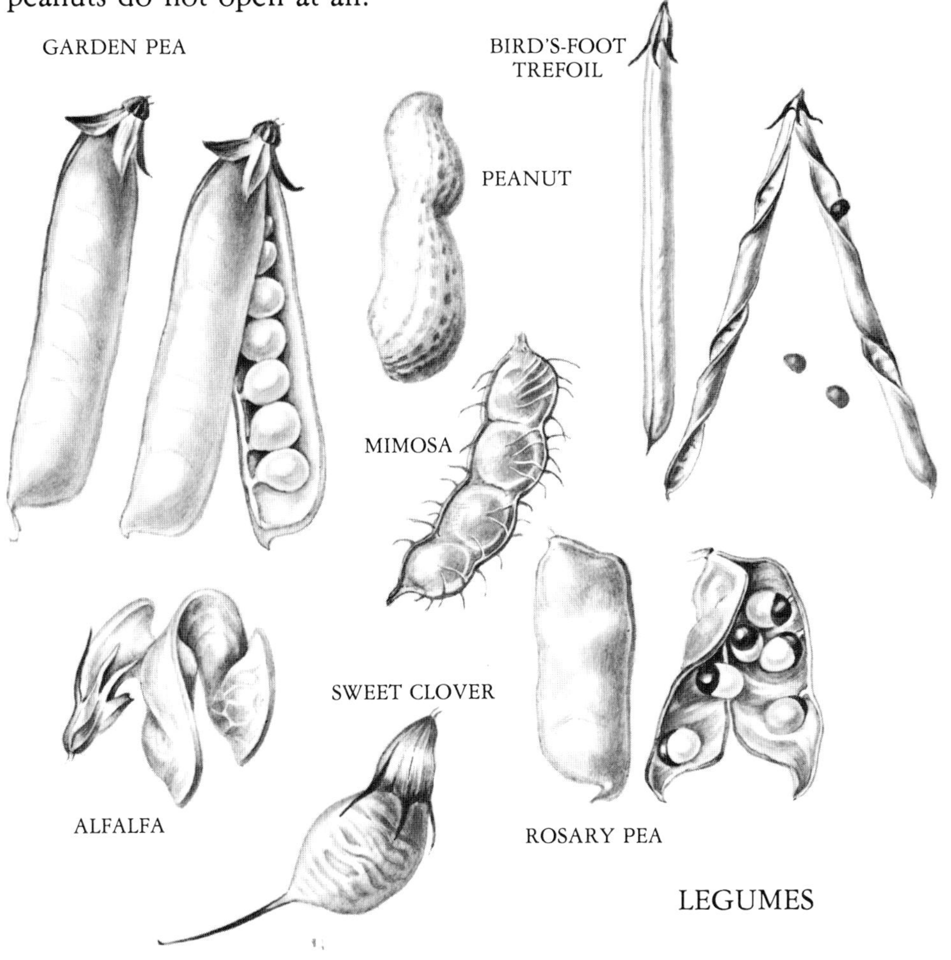

LEGUMES

Not surprisingly, compound pistils develop into the most remarkable variety of fruit forms, with many methods of releasing seeds. Sometimes the carpels merely separate from each other when the fruit is ripe, as in mountain laurel. Sometimes the carpels split down the centers of their backs, as in iris and lily. Sometimes, as in campion, they separate only at their upper tips, so that the fruits look like little vases with small openings at the top through which the seeds can be shaken out. The poppy fruit has very small holes hidden under the edges of its cap (the remains of the stigma), and its tiny black seeds escape through these holes like grains from a saltshaker.

MOUNTAIN LAUREL

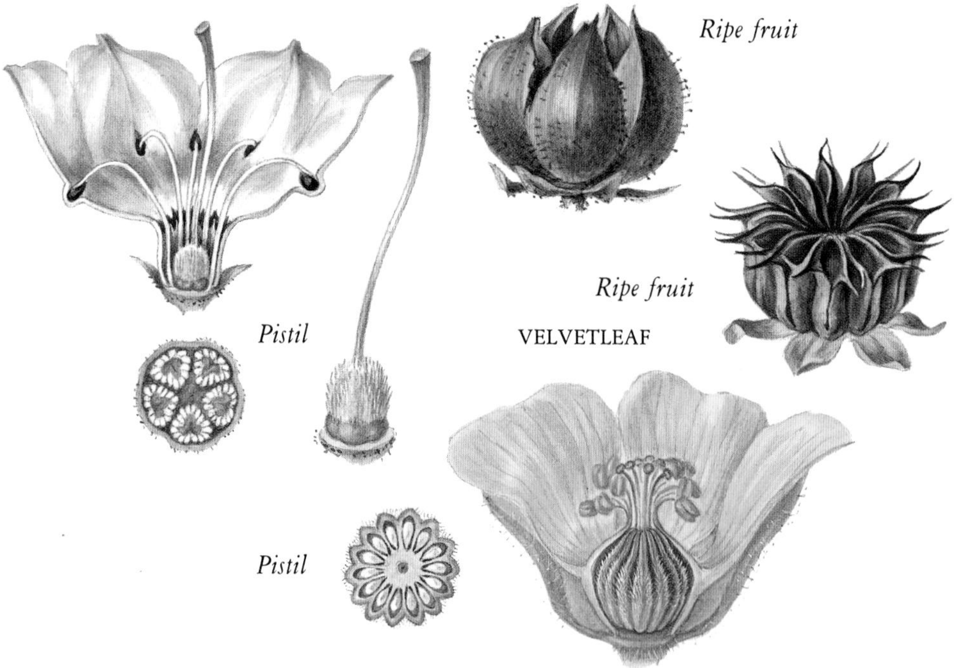

Ripe fruit

Pistil

Ripe fruit

VELVETLEAF

Pistil

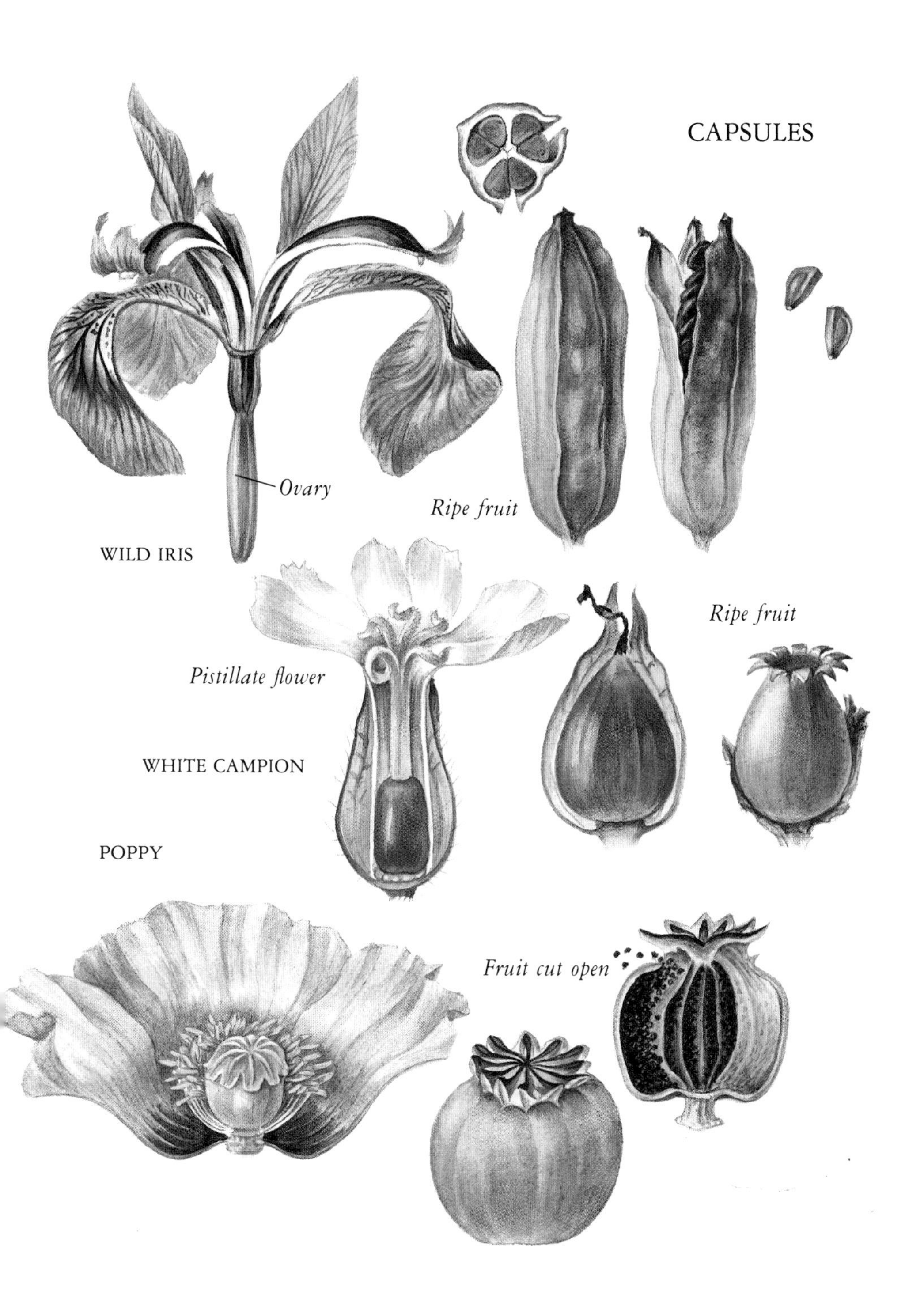
CAPSULES
Ovary
Ripe fruit
WILD IRIS
Ripe fruit
Pistillate flower
WHITE CAMPION
POPPY
Fruit cut open

THE PYXIS

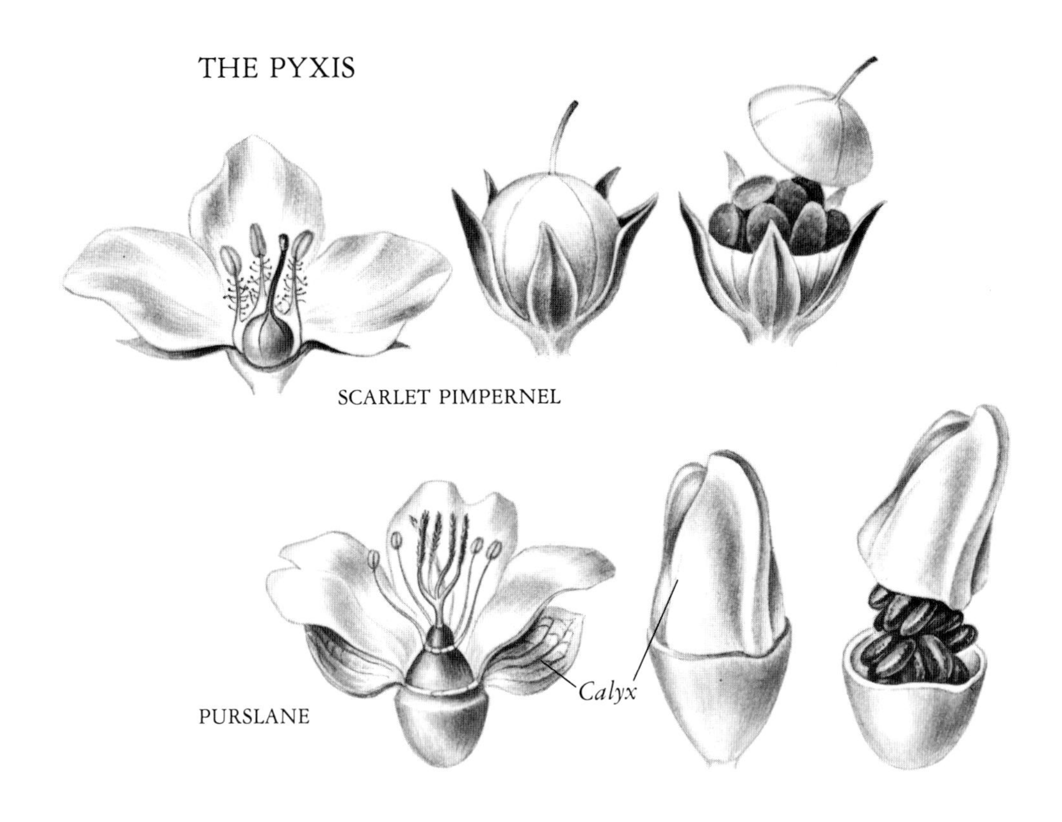

SCARLET PIMPERNEL

PURSLANE

All these multicarpel fruits, in spite of their variations, are called *capsules.* But there are two kinds of capsules different enough to have names of their own—the *pyxis,* which is like a little jar with a removable lid, and the *silique*, typical fruit of the mustard family. A silique has, between its two carpels, a thin membrane bearing seeds on both edges. To release the seeds, the two carpels split apart from the bottom up, leaving the central partition intact, with seeds hanging along its edges. Many siliques are long and narrow, as in mustard and toothwort; but some plants, like pennycress and shepherd's purse, have a short, round type called a *silicle.*

All these various capsular fruits open when it is time for their seeds to go forth into the world. In some cases the seeds drop to the ground or are thrown a short distance as the plant is jostled by an animal or shaken by the wind. But many seed pods have devices that really scatter seeds—sometimes send ing them far away from the mother plant.

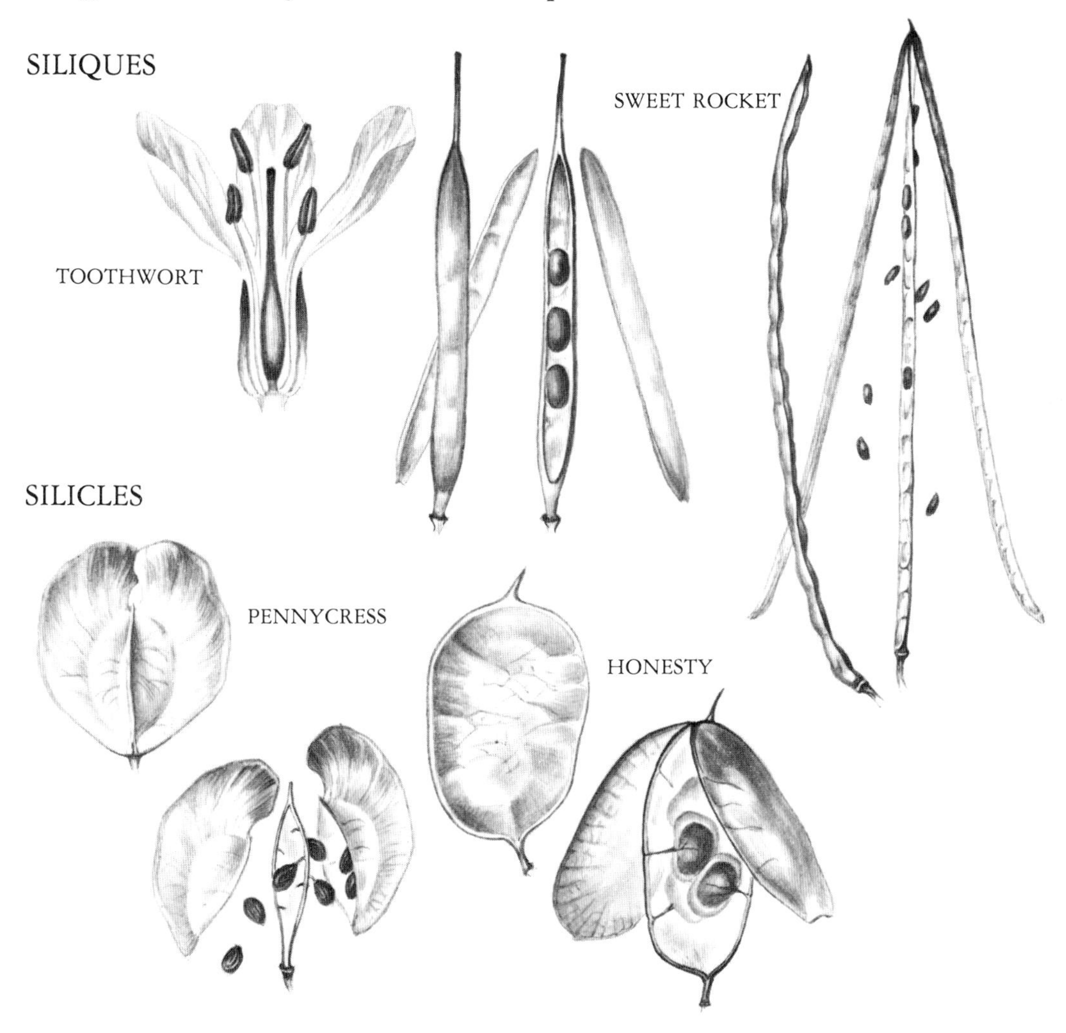

MEADOW VIOLET
Pistil
Fruit
GAS PLANT
Fruit
Pistil
Fruit
Pistil
JEWELWEED

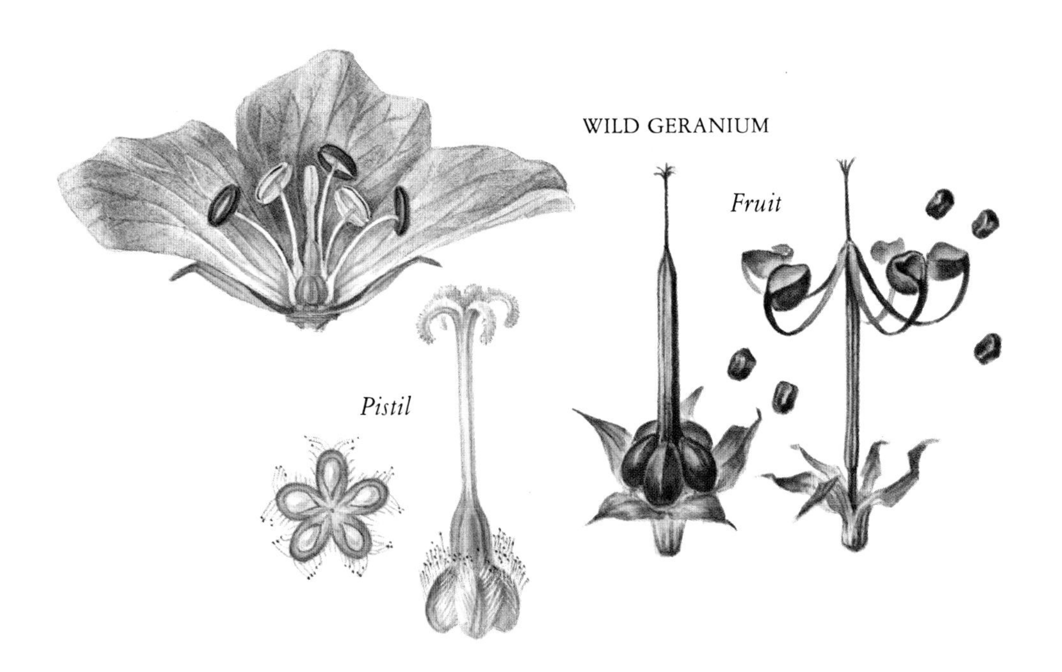

The pods of violets, when ripe and dry, snap open with a little pop that sends a shower of small seeds in all directions; and gas plant capsules, larger and heavier, fire their seeds off with an even louder cannonade. Jewelweed pods toss seeds when even the lightest touch causes them to break apart suddenly and coil up like springs. They are so sensitive that the plant has two alternate names—impatiens and touch-me-not.

Wild geranium, or cranesbill, gets one of its names from the very prominent beak that tops its seed capsule. This beak is the style of the pistil. It has persisted and grown along with the ovary, and when the fruit is ripe, beak and carpels split apart, snap up and out, and literally throw the five seeds in all directions.

Many dry fruits travel far afield by enlisting the aid of moving agents. Some hitch rides by means of spines or hooks

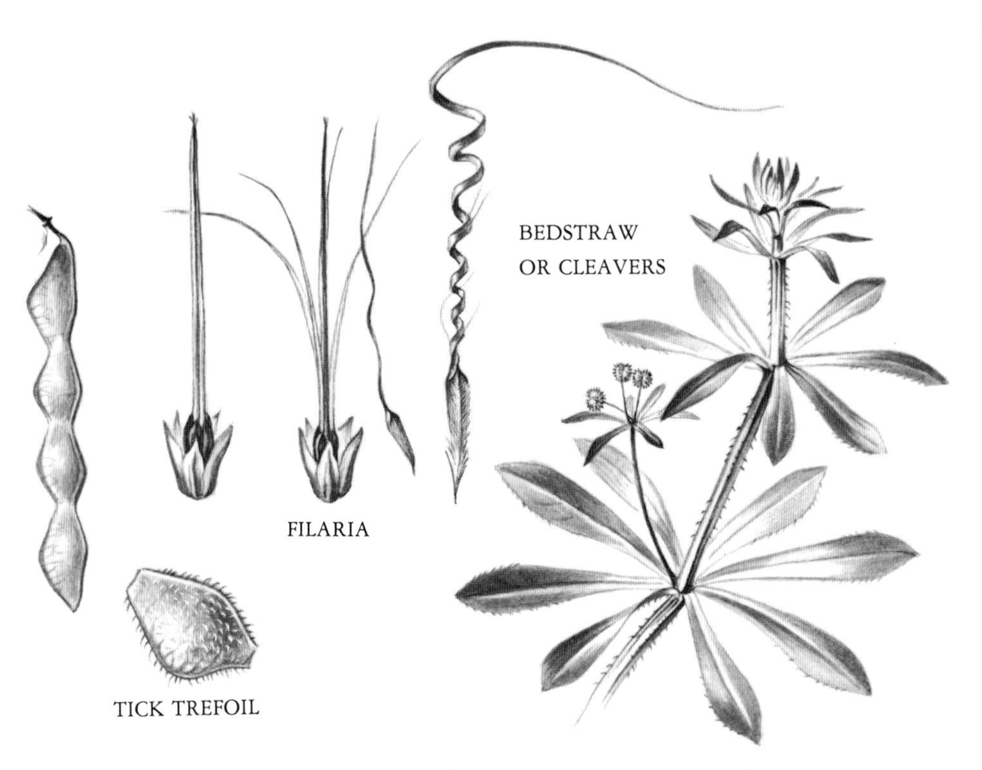

that catch in the hair of animals or the clothing of people. The legumes of tick trefoil, densely covered with minute barbed hairs, break crosswise, and the pieces stick tightly to anything that touches them. The ripe fruits of filaria split into sections much like those of its relative, geranium, but each pointed carpel has a long tail that twists into a perfect spiral. It responds to moisture, uncoiling when wet and re-coiling tightly when dry, and thus it actually screws the fruit into the fur of animals or, eventually, plants it firmly in the ground.

Sometimes a whole plant becomes an agent of distribution. Several species of bedstraw are called cleavers because their stems and leaves are covered with tiny hooked hairs. They catch on—cleave to—anything that passes, and pieces of the plant are broken off and carried away. The tumbleweeds of the west, which have evolved in dry, open country, break from their roots and roll along before the wind, dropping seeds as they go. A number of quite different species do this—Russian thistle, pigweed, tumble mustard—and they all scatter seeds by the millions.

Water also can be a dispersing agent. Lightweight pods and seeds are often borne along on country streams. The little fruits of silverweed can float for months to new homes on riverbanks, and coconuts are famous for the long ocean voyages they often make before they are cast up on island shores.

All these devices have enabled the flowering plants to inherit the earth. The ones with the most efficient means of seed distribution will most quickly move into any new sites that are opened up for them. There they face a struggle to establish themselves, governed by many factors: their own adaptability and length of life, the number of seeds they produce, the amount of nutrient in the seeds, and the seeds' ability to survive and germinate.

TUMBLEWEEDS

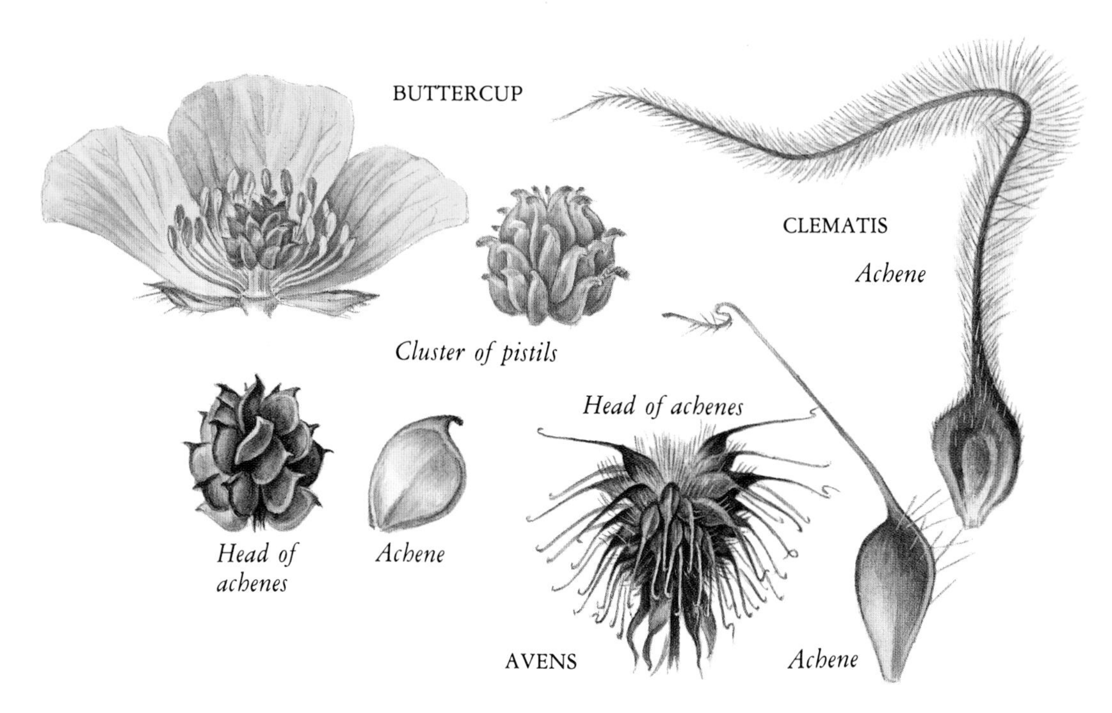

DRY FRUITS THAT DO NOT OPEN

A great many dry fruits do not split open to release their seeds, and they are somewhat different in structure from those that do, even though they may grow from ovaries that seem almost identical. The buttercup flower, with its cluster of many one-carpel pistils, is very much like a marsh marigold flower. Its pistils ripen into a similar seed head, but each of them, instead of becoming a follicle, develops into a small hard fruit called an *achene*, with the thin pericarp fitting snugly around the one seed inside it. When ripe, each achene breaks separately from the cluster; dry and hard, it can easily be mistaken for a simple seed.

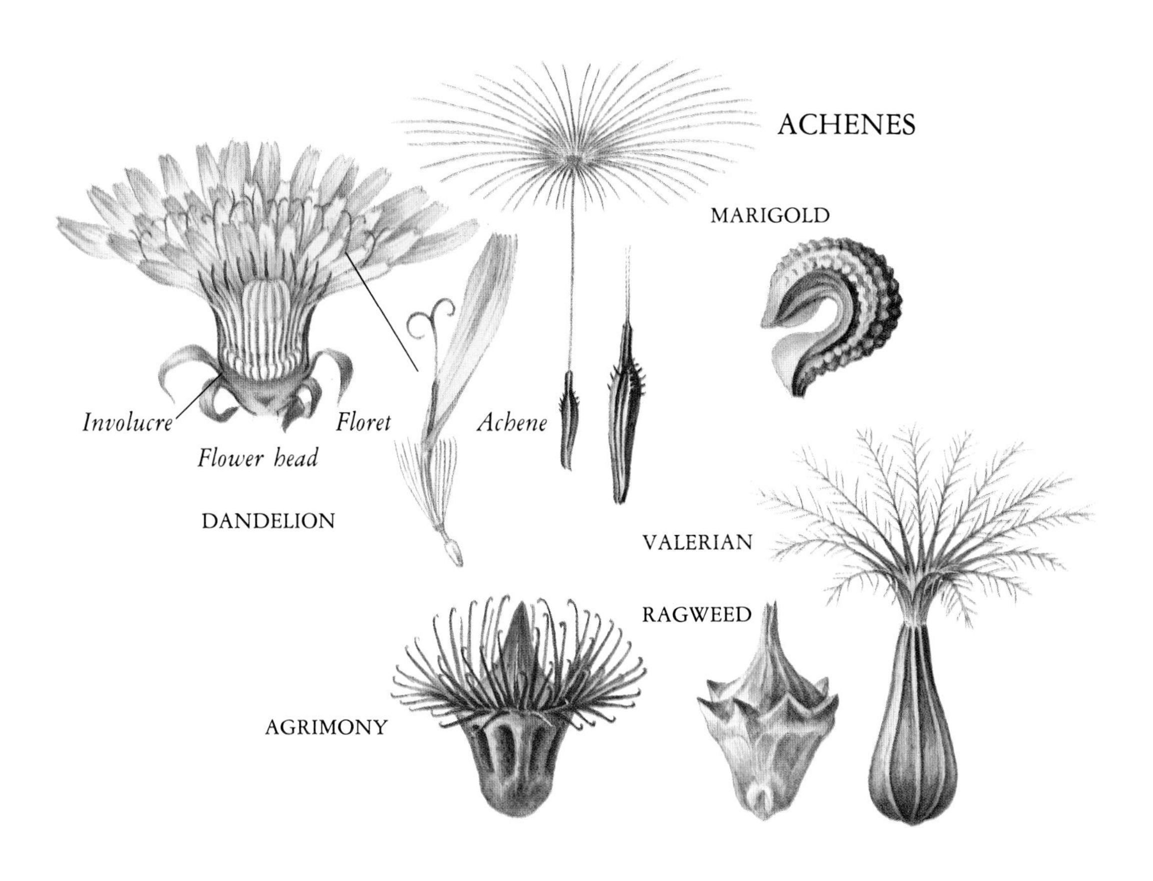

Achenes often have interesting shapes and ridged surfaces. Their basic forms are generally those of the ovaries that preceded them, but often other flower parts persist and become parts of the fruit, usually as devices for distribution. In fact, achenes have a remarkable array of special equipment for getting around in the world. In avens fruits the stigma and style remain on the achene as a long barbed hook; in clematis and pasqueflower they grow into a feathery plume. In the daisy family it is the calyx of small hairs that becomes the well-known parachute on the achenes of dandelion, thistle, and aster or the spiky crown on those of sneezeweed and

ACHENES

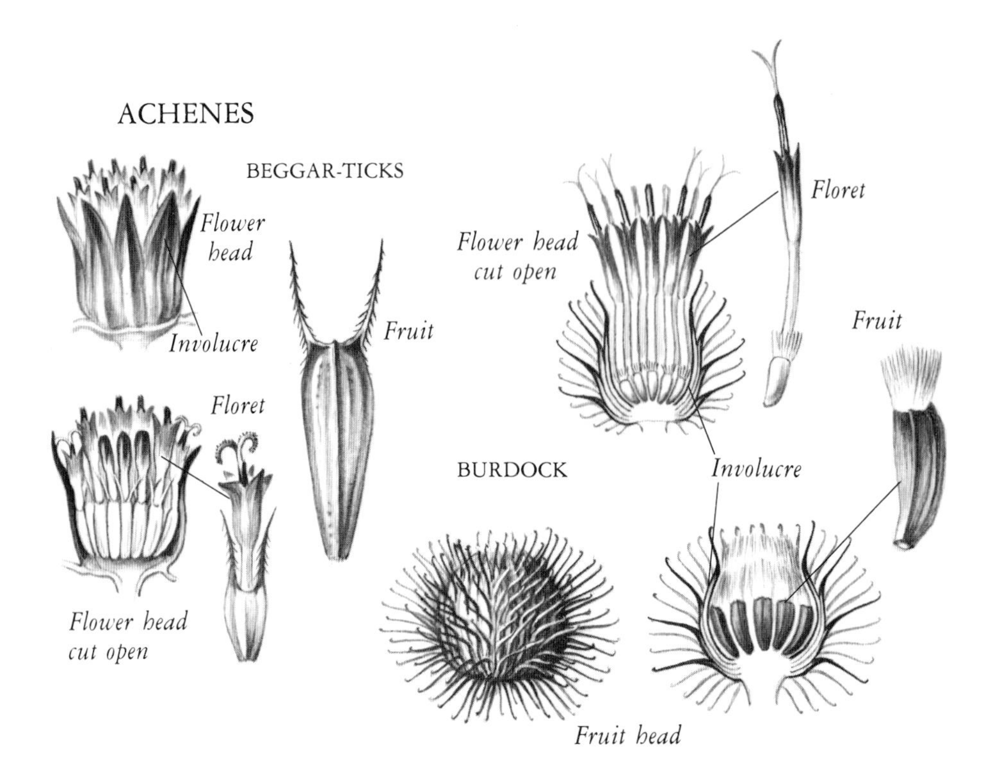

cornflower. In beggar-ticks, that calyx develops into several barbed spikes. Still another flower part forms the spiny burr of burdock and cocklebur—the *involucre*, a cup of tiny leaves or scales that surrounds the flower head in every member of the daisy family. In burdock, the involucre almost completely encloses the achenes, and the sharp barbs on its scales are an extremely efficient means of distributing them.

Some nonsplitting fruits could not possibly be distinguished from achenes, or even from bare seeds, by anyone who did not know their inner structure. A *grain* (sometimes called a *caryopsis*) is almost exactly like an achene, except that its pericarp has become completely fused with its one seed. All members of the grass family produce grains, born from tiny flowers in clusters that may be as small and delicate as that of panic grass or as big and solid as an ear of corn. An enormous number of them have hairs or spines or barbs to help in seed distribution, but most of these spines are on the tiny scales that enclose the fruits, not on the fruits themselves. Several species have at the tips of their scales very long bristles or *awns*, bent near the middle and twisted below, much like the tails of filaria fruits. The awns react to moisture in exactly the same way, and push the fruits forward with the same screwing action.

GRAINS

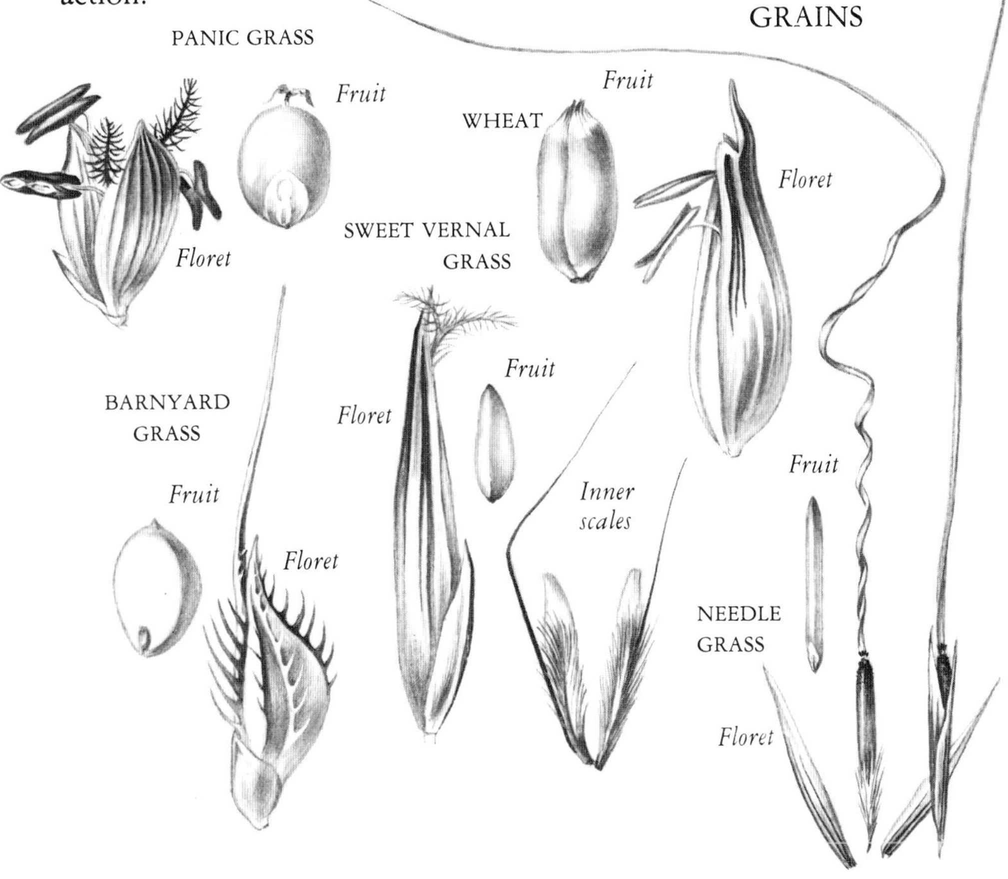

NUTS

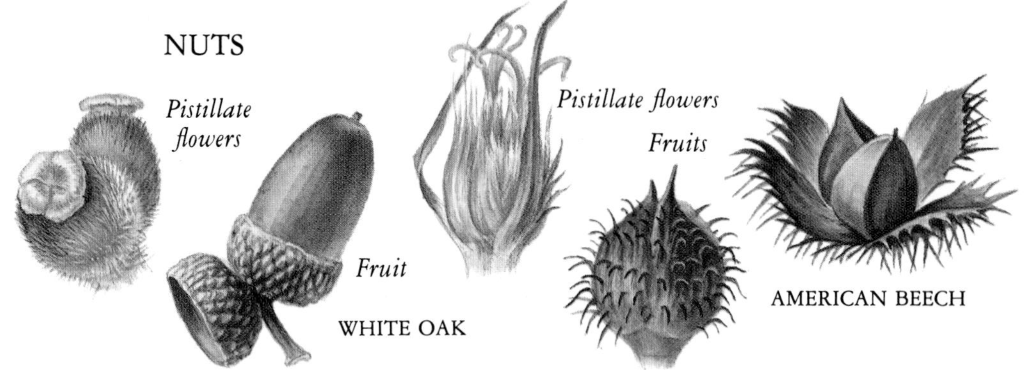

A *nut* is also very like an achene, since it is a one-seeded fruit with a leathery or stony pericarp. But nuts are likely to be at least partly enclosed by an involucre, which may be a rough cup like the oak's, a spiny case like the beech's, a hard shell like the hickory's, or a leafy envelope like the hazelnut's. Nuts have no built-in devices for seed distribution. If not interfered with, they drop heavily to the ground and eventually grow where they fall. But often they are interfered with, especially by squirrels, which carry them off, bury them, and frequently forget them.

Another kind of hard, nonopening fruit with one seed is

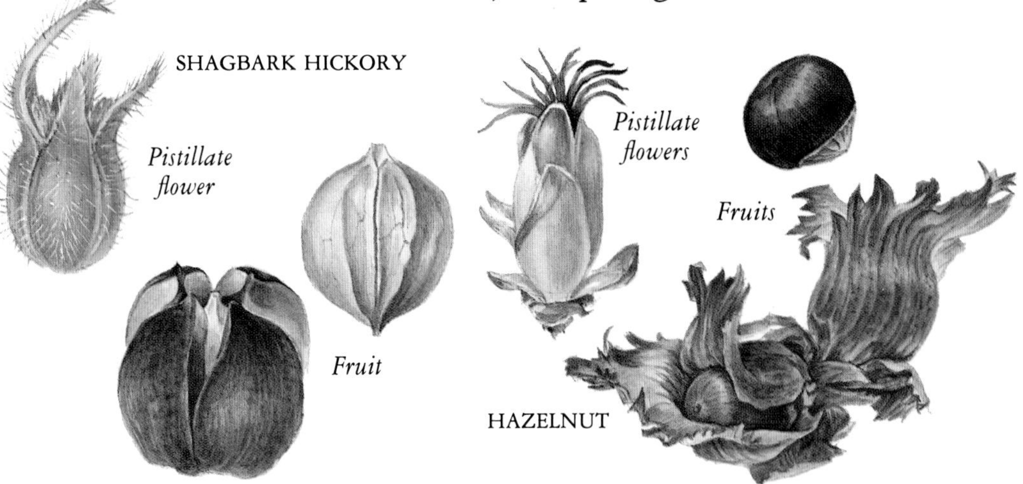

basically an achene, but it has wings and is called a *samara.* A great many trees, such as elm and ash, bear samaras and launch them from high branches like fleets of little gliders. On ailanthus, they grow in great masses, and on windy days the ripe fruits fly so wildly that it is no wonder this tree has become a weed. The familiar keys of the maple are slightly different in structure; each grows from a two-carpel ovary and becomes a pair of one-seeded samaras joined in the middle. The halves break apart during, or soon after, their flight.

The fruits of the parsley family also split into two halves, each half hard and one seeded like an achene. They are called

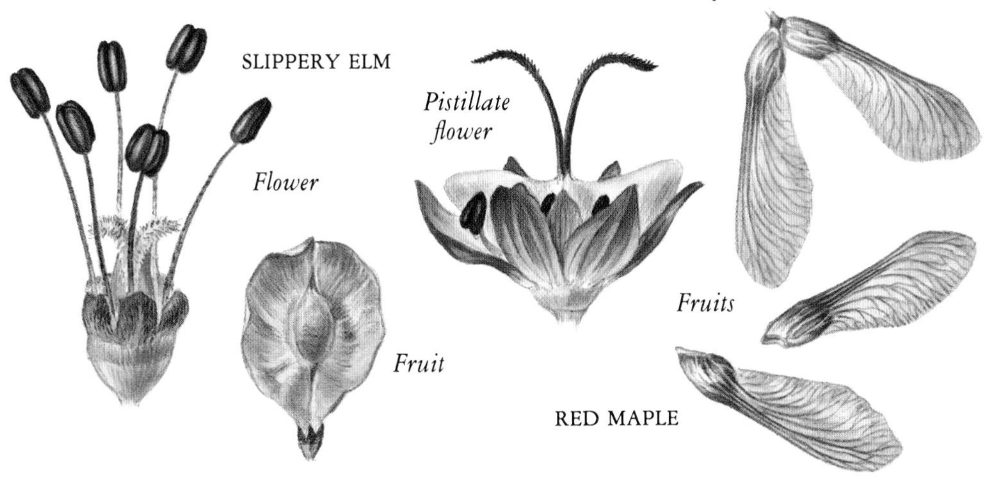

schizocarps, and they have a very distinctive appearance, with their two halves hanging from a central axis. They also have a great variety of shapes, with many elaborate bristles or ridges or fins.

Of all this multitude of dry fruits—those that open and those that do not—perhaps the majority will never find a place on grocery shelves, even though most of them are eaten by birds or mammals. Nevertheless, a great many do provide food for man, and in enormous quantities. All our cereals are grains from the grass family, and one of them—wheat—supplies mankind with more food than any other plant or animal product, with rice a close second. The seeds of legumes—beans and their relatives—are next in importance. Nearly all nuts are edible, and so are sunflower "seeds" (really achenes). And from the schizocarps of the parsley family come many of our best-known flavorings: caraway, anise, coriander, and dozens of others.

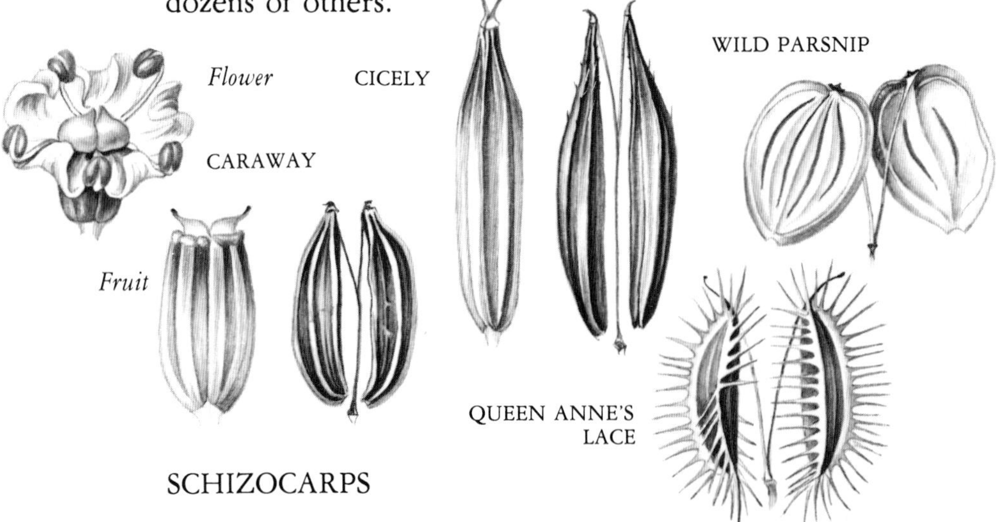

SCHIZOCARPS

TOMATO

FLESHY FRUITS

To most of us, "edible fruits" are fleshy fruits—the ones with succulent pericarps, usually sweet and juicy, and tempting to both man and animal. Sweet temptation is often the only device these fruits have for seed dispersal. They are carried about by creatures that want to eat them; sometimes the seeds are discarded as the fruit is devoured; often they pass unharmed through the creature's digestive tract.

Fleshy fruits, of course, all develop from flower ovaries just as dry fruits do. They grow from both simple and compound pistils, and they may contain one seed or hundreds. The ovary walls, instead of becoming thin and brittle, develop into a pericarp that is mostly pulp, enclosed in a skin or rind.

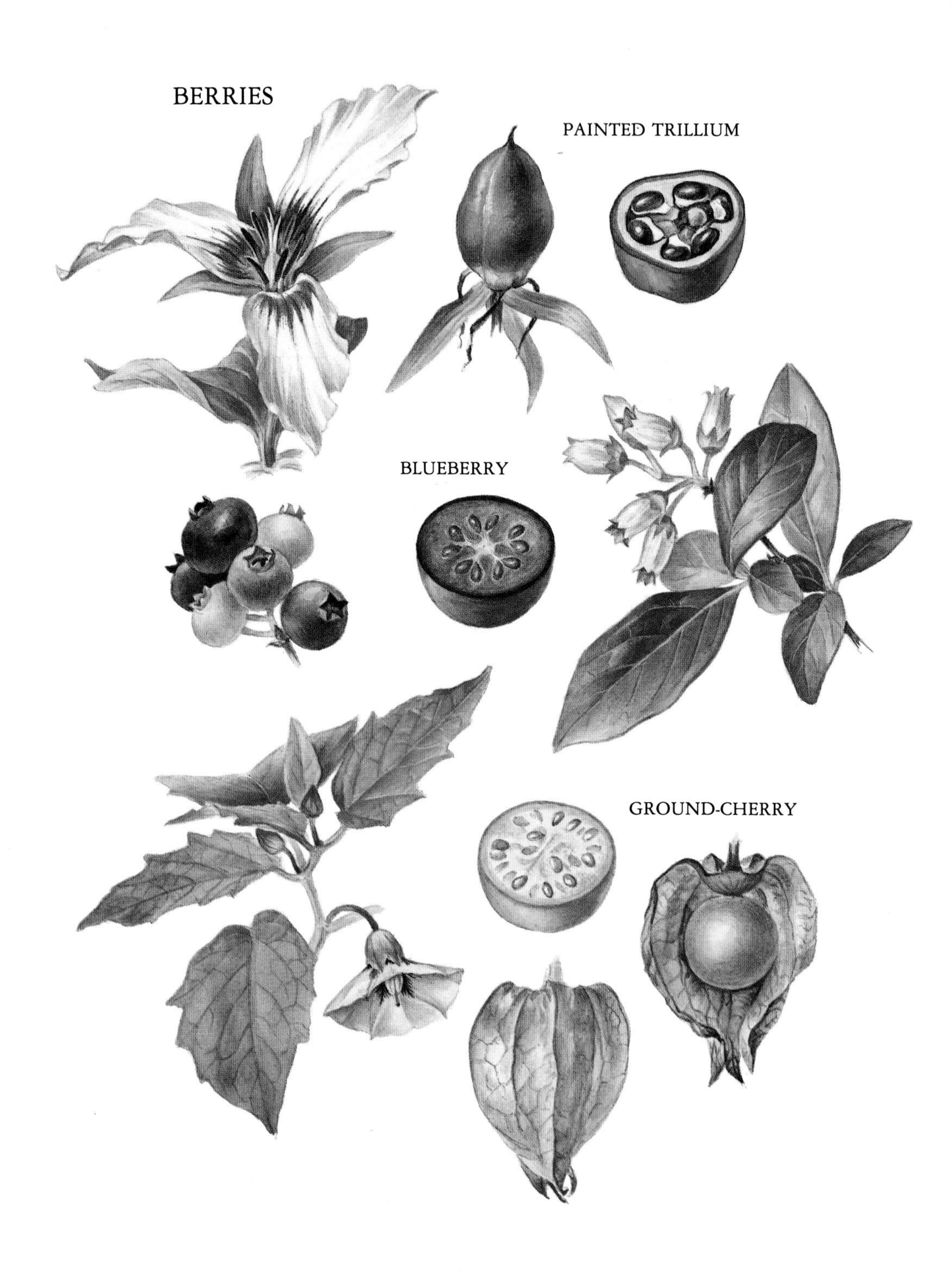
BERRIES
PAINTED TRILLIUM
BLUEBERRY
GROUND-CHERRY

The simplest of the fleshy fruits is the *berry*, with its seeds—one or many—surrounded by pulp inside a thin skin. Grapes, blueberries, and currants are obvious berries, but there are others we would not commonly call by that name—tomato, banana, eggplant, and date, for example. Berries occur in many plant families and develop from the ovaries of flowers of all shapes and sizes: the small bells of the blueberry, the lilylike blooms of the trillium, the strange little knobs enclosed in a jack-in-the-pulpit. Grapes grow from tiny blossoms that drop their petals as they open, and the big avocado fruit comes from a very small greenish flower that has no petals. The ground-cherry flower has a calyx that expands to become a balloonlike case completely enclosing the berry.

Pumpkins, squashes, and cucumbers are a variation of the berry type called a *pepo*; and another variation is the *hesperidium* of the orange, lemon, and grapefruit.

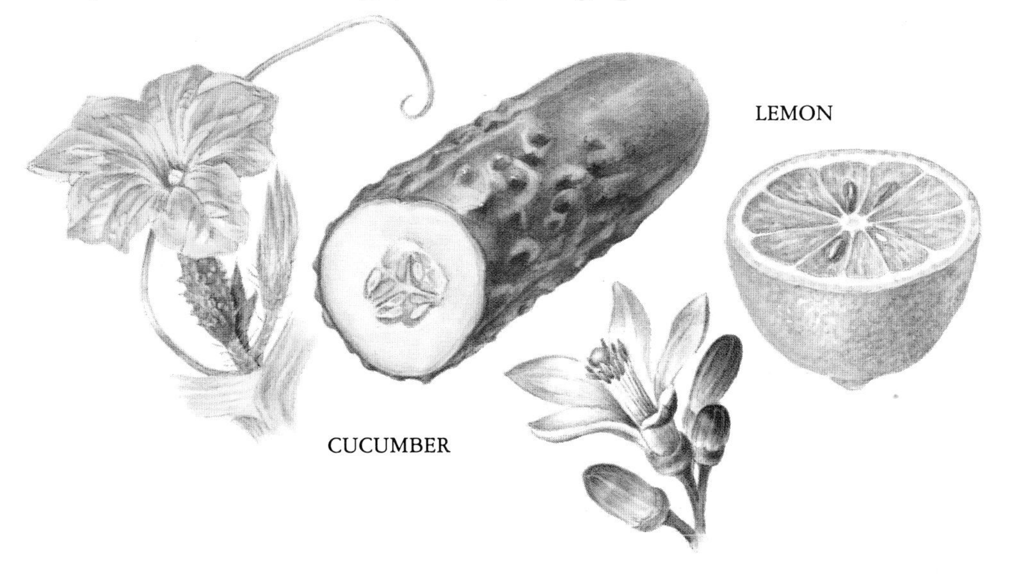

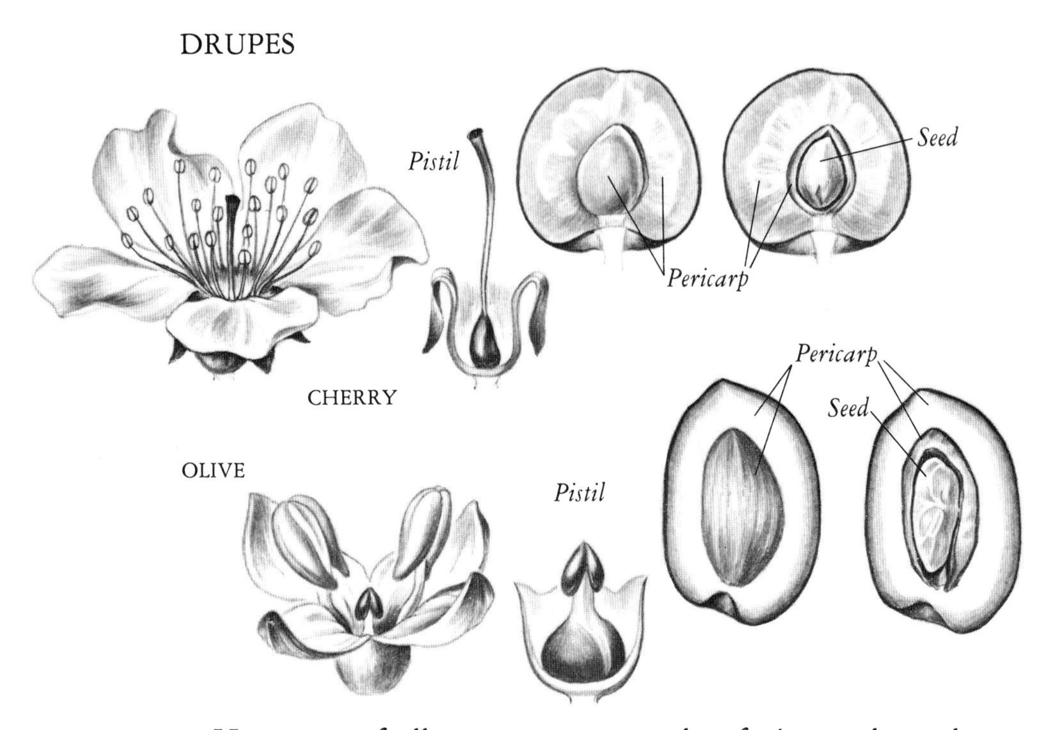

However, of all our common market fruits, perhaps the greatest number are *drupes*, like cherries, peaches, and plums. The skin of the pericarp and the fleshy layer inside the skin are much like those of a berry, but the innermost layer of the pericarp is hard and bony. This layer is the "stone" of the peach or the "pit" of the cherry, seeming more a part of the seed it encloses than a part of the juicy pericarp. Drupes are often called "stone fruits," and they include a great variety of kinds: Mangos and olives are drupes, and so are coconuts, though their flesh has become fibrous rather than juicy. In the case of drupes like walnuts and almonds, we do not eat the fleshy part of the pericarp, but break through its bony inner layer (the shell of the "nut"), and eat the seed inside it.

Therefore almonds and walnuts are not true nuts.

Cherries, plums, peaches, and almonds are members of the rose family. The flowers of this large and interesting group are all very much alike, but they produce a remarkable array of differing fruit types. They well illustrate the kind of variations that occur when an ovary is joined by other flower parts as it develops into a fruit. In this family the crucial part is the receptacle, which varies surprisingly from species to species. In the cherry it is a shallow cup, with the simple pistil sitting in the middle of it, and it disappears as the fruit develops. In

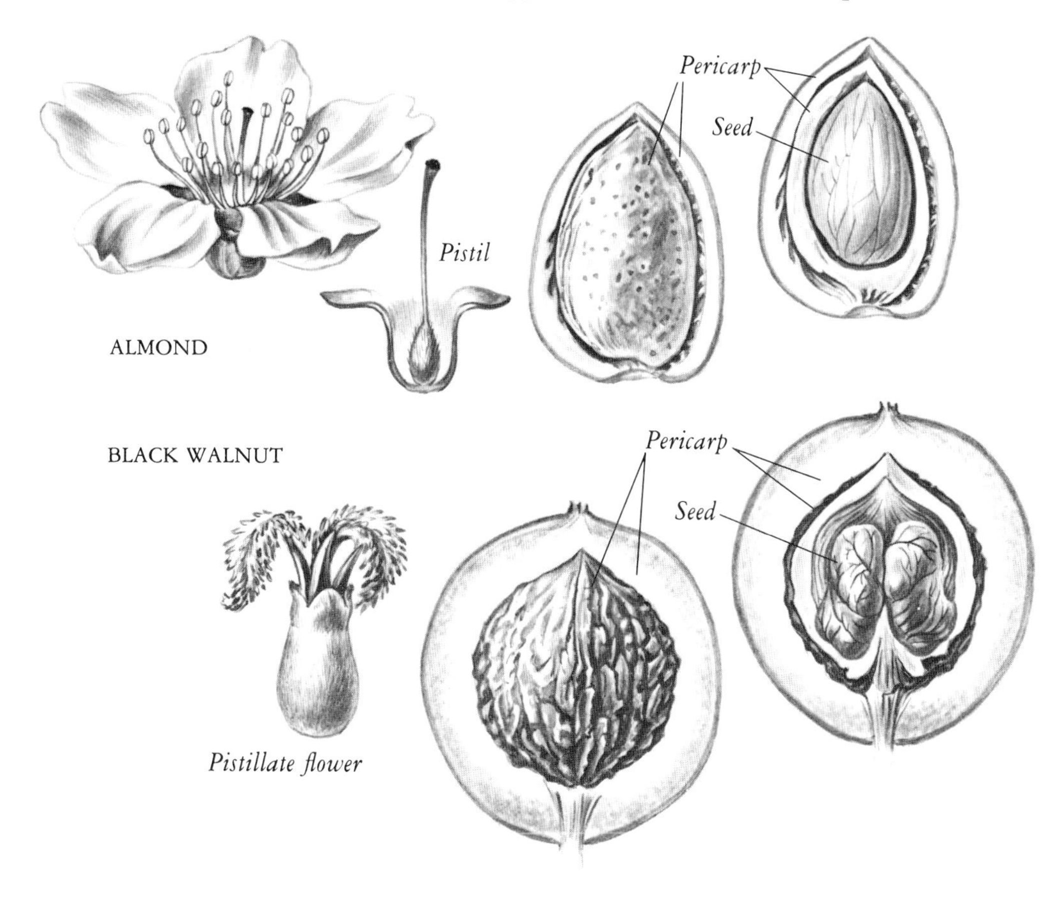

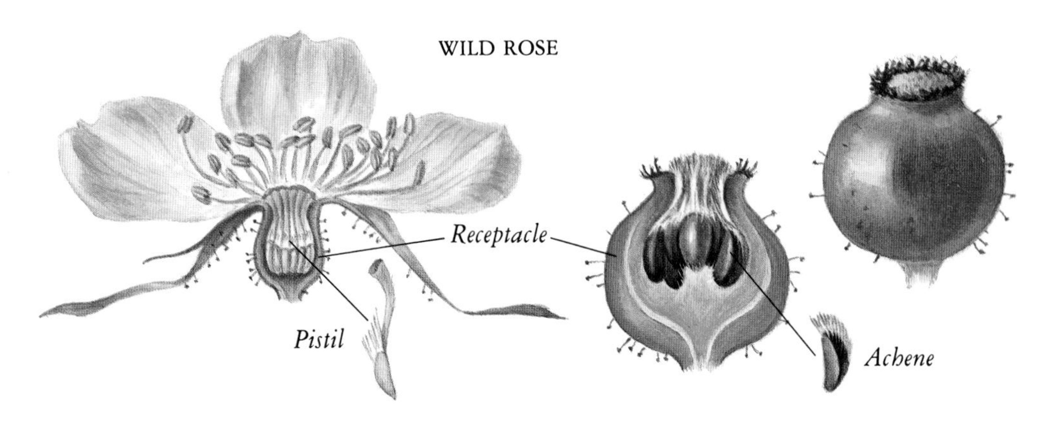

a rose flower the receptacle is a deep cup with a small opening, enclosing a cluster of separate pistils. As the pistils grow, the cup around them grows too, becoming the bright and succulent rose "hip" that looks like a vase, holding a number of hard fruits or achenes. In the flower of apple or pear the cup-shaped receptacle is closed at the top, completely surrounding the compound ovary. As the ovary ripens, its ovules become brown seeds, and the inner walls of its five carpels become translucent, gristly sacs around them: the core of the apple. Around all this, and merging with it, is the receptacle,

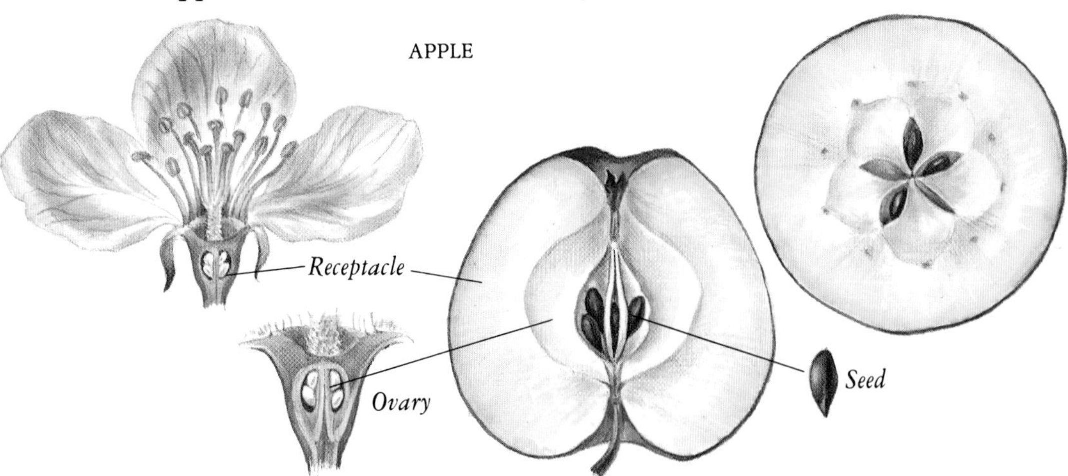

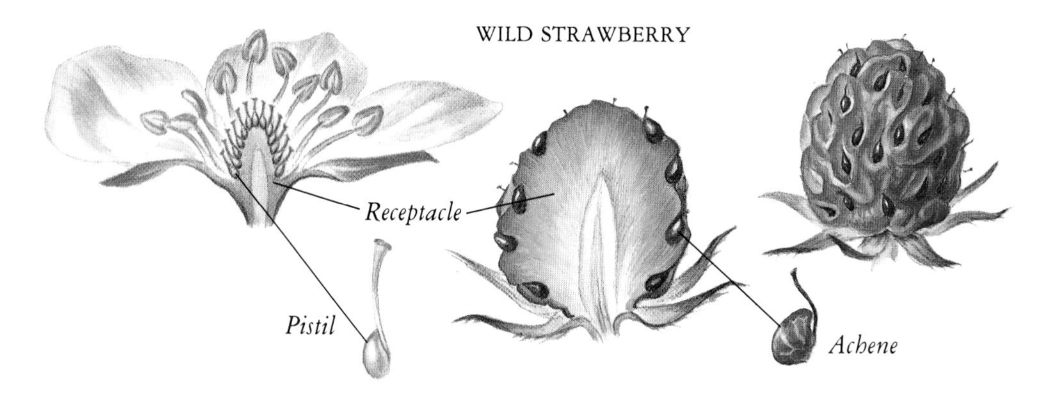

now grown large and edible—a fruit called a *pome.*

In strawberry flowers the receptacle is a mound or cone with a large number of simple pistils growing on its surface. The pistils ripen into small hard achenes, but the receptacle on which they perch grows enormously, till it becomes the red and tasty part we eat. The parts of a blackberry flower almost exactly match those of the strawberry, but they develop quite differently. Though the blackberry receptacle does get bigger, it remains a core, and the ovaries on its surface become the sweet and edible segments of the fruit—

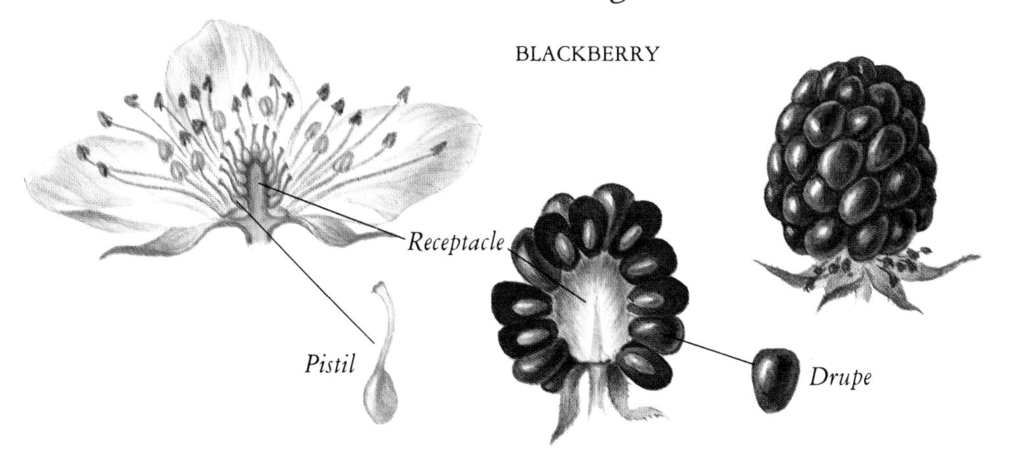

they are a cluster of tiny drupes rather than achenes.

Strawberries and blackberries are obviously not berries to a botanist. They are, however, good examples of the *aggregate fruit*, a type produced by the joining of a number of pistils that were separate in a flower.

A *multiple fruit* is composed of separate pistils from separate flowers. The mulberry, for instance, looks very much like a blackberry, but it is derived from a cluster of tiny flowers, and each of its juicy segments is the combined calyx and pistil of a separate floret. A pineapple fruit is a whole big head of flowers fused together, along with all their parts and the stalk they grew on. A fig is a large receptacle—a pouch completely enclosing hundreds of very small florets. In some fig receptacles there are both staminate and pistillate flowers, with the staminate ones near the mouth of the sac, the pistillate ones on the sides and bottom; in others, there are only pistillate

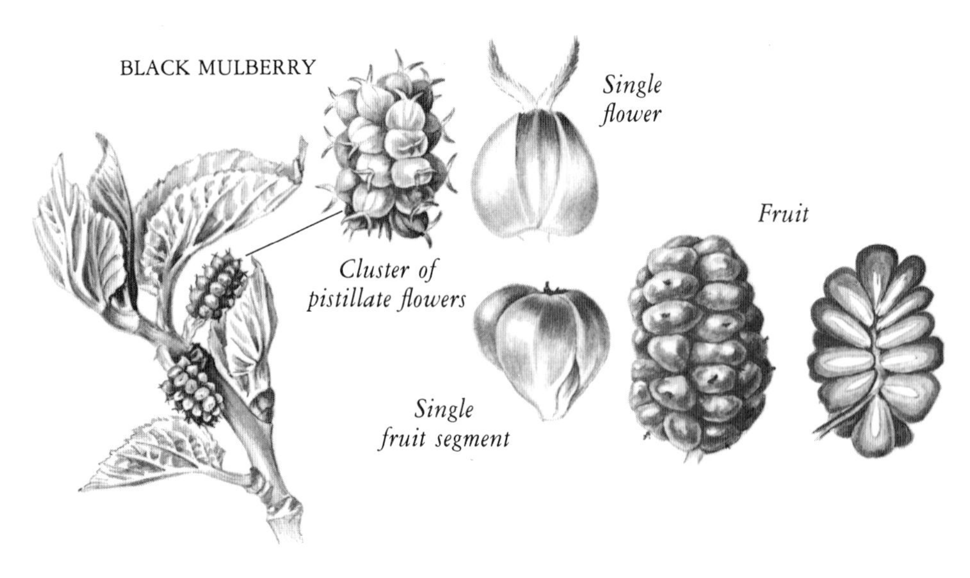

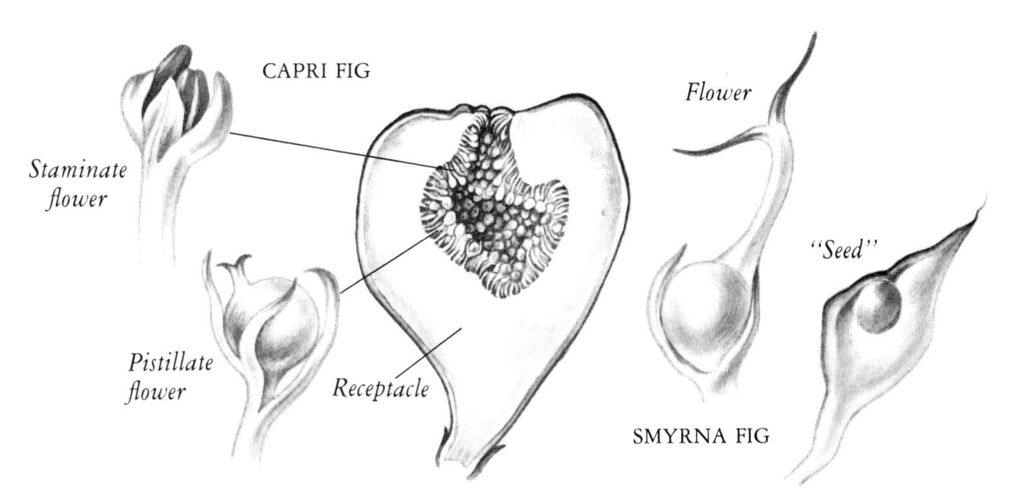

flowers. All wild figs are pollinated by wasps so tiny that they can crawl into the receptacle, but some cultivated figs produce fruits without any pollination.

And, in contrast to all that complexity, the little double fruits of the wild partridgeberry are the combined ovaries and receptacles of only a pair of blossoms. But they too are multiple fruits.

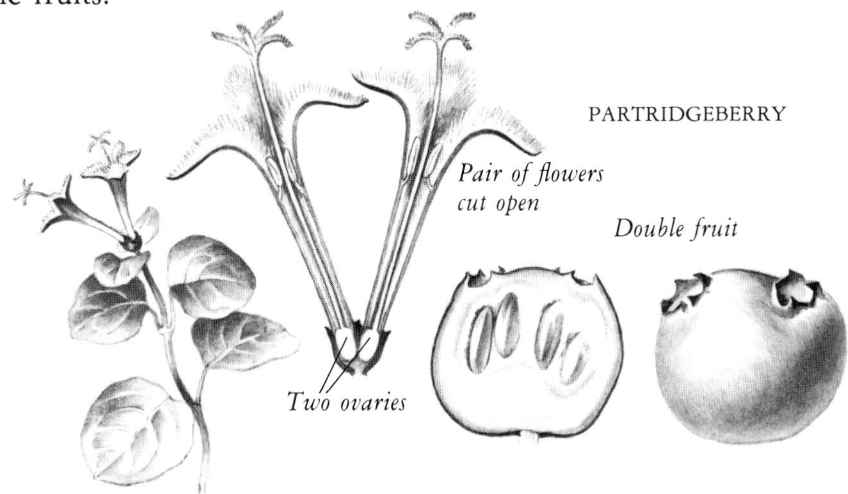

MULTIPLE FRUITS

TYPICAL EMBRYOS

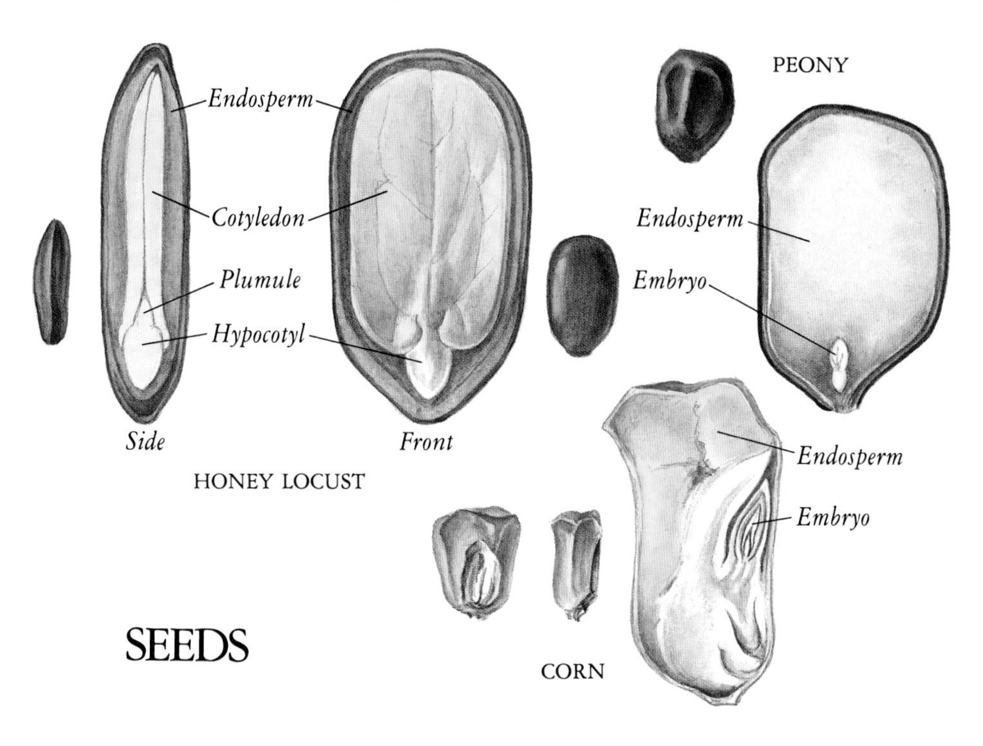

SEEDS

All this multitude of fruits—simple or complex, edible or inedible—would have no reason for being if it were not for the precious seeds inside them, those bits of packaged energy that carry the future of their species and even the future of the whole green world.

As soon as an ovule is fertilized, a new life is conceived and changes begin. Each ovule soon becomes a tiny new plant enclosed in a container that will keep it safe until it reaches a time and place where it can make its connection with the earth and become able to support itself. The integuments of the ovule become the coats of the seed, usually a hard outer one and a membranous inner one. The cells inside reorganize themselves as the embryo takes shape and the endosperm develops. Often the baby plants are so minute that they occupy only part of the space in even the smallest seeds, and all around them is the endosperm—the mass of starch and protein and oil that will provide nourishment when growing starts. But sometimes, as in the sunflower or the locust, the plump embryo fills the whole space, having already absorbed all the food into its seed leaves. These little embryos seldom look much like plants. Each has one or two very simple leaves, the *cotyledons*; a bud or growing point, the *plumule*; and a short stem or *hypocotyl*, from which a root, or *radicle*, will eventually descend.

There are almost as many different kinds of seeds in the world as there are kinds of plants. The largest ones known are a foot long and weigh forty pounds, while others are so small

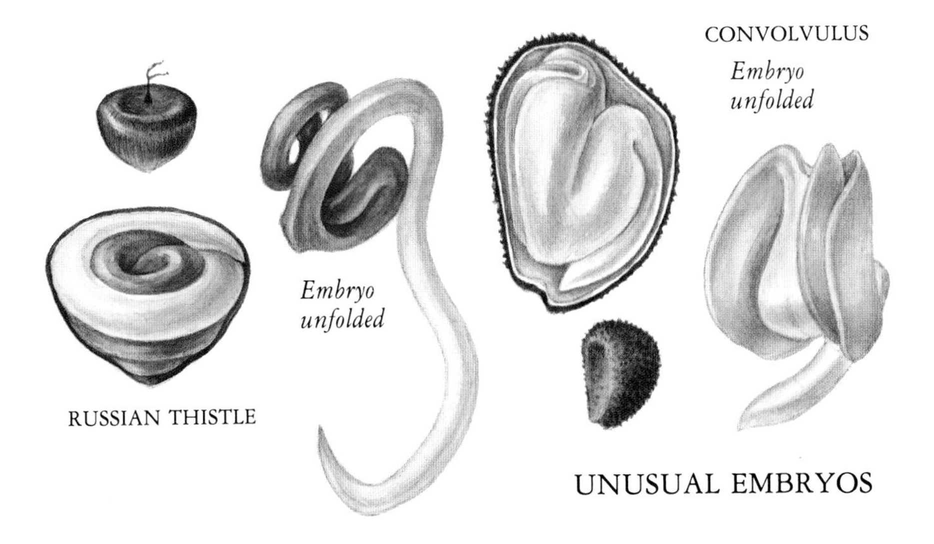

UNUSUAL EMBRYOS

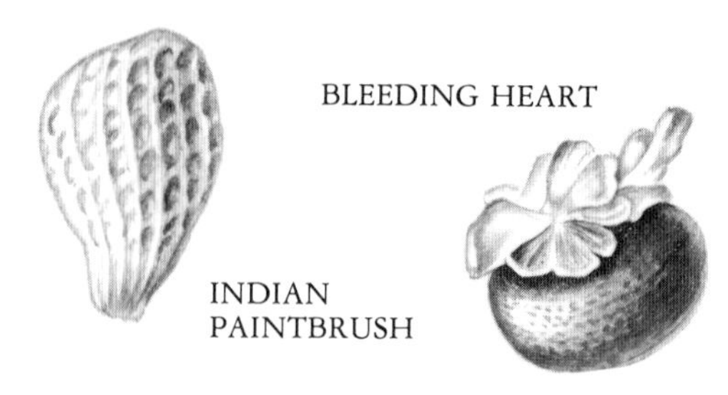

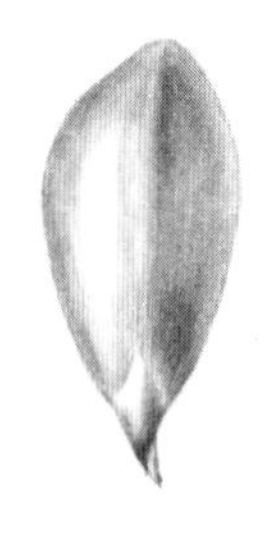

that it takes 137 million of them to weigh one pound. But large or small, the seed must have an outer coat that is tough and waterproof, and often extremely hard. It may be smooth and shiny, or corrugated, or patterned, or decorated with wings or hairs. Sometimes these hairs form parachutes similar to the ones that carry the achenes of dandelion or thistle. Milkweed parachutes ride the wind for miles, and poplar seeds can fill the air with flying "cotton." (The seeds of true cotton are covered with dense white fibers, sometimes two inches long, that have been used for weaving cloth since the days of the ancient Egyptians.) Lily seeds are light enough to be carried by the wind, and so are those with wings. Seeds can also travel, as fruits do, in the fur of animals, and very often on the feet of birds. They cling by means of their own sticky coating or are, more commonly, caught in mud. Whole weed gardens have been grown from seeds found on the feet of migrating birds.

Fertilized ovules, and the fruits enclosing them, continue to develop until the seeds are ripe. Then the seeds stop growing and settle down to wait for conditions that will make it possible for them to *germinate* and grow into new plants. This waiting period can vary enormously—from a few days to thousands of years. Some maple seeds die when they dry out,

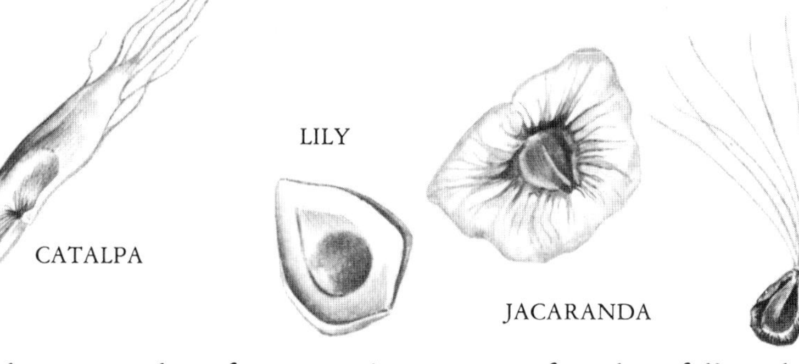

MILKWEED

and they must therefore germinate soon after they fall to the ground. Orchid seeds are so minute that they carry no food supply, and they must germinate almost immediately upon their release. On the other hand, living lotus seeds, found in a Manchurian bog, were proved to be 1000 years old; and lupine seeds found frozen underground in Canada grew into healthy plants even though they were 10,000 years old. Of course, both these extremes are very rare, and the seeds of most plants wait a few months or a few years. The maximum for fancy garden seeds is usually a year or two; but those of various wild plants can rest anywhere from five years to ninety.

SQUASH

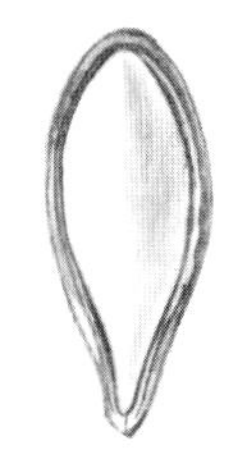

This waiting period is called *dormancy*, and when it begins, the seed goes into a kind of sleep. It dries out and appears to be dead—in fact, its life processes slow to the point where they can scarcely be measured at all. Dormancy is a very important device for the survival of seeds. In the first place, they have to wait while they find a suitable spot to grow in; once there, they must continue to wait for favorable germinating conditions. Since it is obviously an advantage for baby plants to start growing in the spring, a great many seeds lie dormant all winter, and many need a certain number of cold and warm days before they can germinate. In the seeds of

GARDEN BEAN

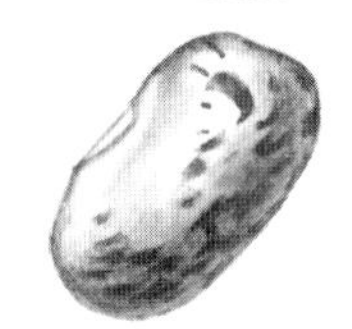

some plants, dormancy allows embryos an additional period of development before they are ready to grow. In many stone fruits the growing embryo cannot penetrate the bony wall around it until that wall has been softened by decay, by passing through an animal's digestive tract, or by soaking, freezing, or scraping. In the desert, seeds wait till a rainy season insures a water supply for the sprouting seedlings. And the seeds of many plants germinate progressively—a season's crop will produce a few plants each year for several years, so that a bad season does not wipe out a whole generation.

And so our seed, fully ripened and safely carried to a new home, lies sleeping in the earth for a few months or a few years, waiting for the conditions that will cause it to awake or germinate. These conditions are many and complex. Light in some cases helps germination, sometimes impedes it. Temperature plays a part, though plants vary greatly in their need for warmth. And oxygen is also very important. But most important of all is water, and in tropical parts of the world, plant growth depends on dry and rainy seasons rather than on the cycle of warmth and cold.

Absorption of water makes the embryo begin to grow, nourished by the food in the endosperm. The first outward sign of germination is a swelling of the whole seed. Then its coat is ruptured and a rootlet appears, groping unerringly downward to bury itself in the earth. Other parts of the embryo lengthen and separate, often lifting the shell of the seed as they reach upward toward the light. Soon the plumule develops its little green leaves, and the seedling at last becomes an independent plant, able to support itself. It is then ready to manufacture its own food, to bear flowers and fruits, and eventually to send out in its turn the seeds that will carry on its species.

GERMINATION OF A LOCUST SEED

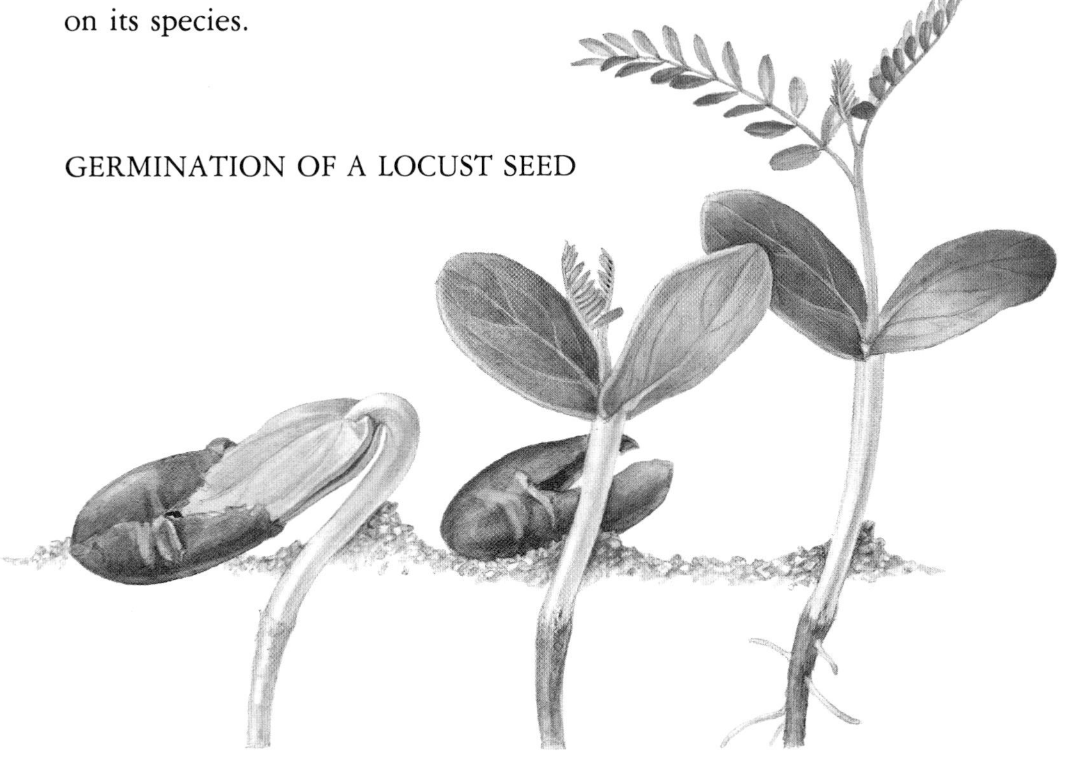

Index of Plants

Page numbers in *italic* indicate illustrations

Subject Index